Empath

The Empath's Guide to Overcoming Social Anxiety as an Empath and Highly Sensitive Person

By: Daniel Patterson

Table of Contents

Chapter 1: What Does It Mean to Be an Empath?................... 5

Chapter 2: Understanding Your Empathic Nature 21

Chapter 3: Blocking Unwanted Thoughts and Emotions..................31

Chapter 4: Cleansing Yourself of Unwanted Energies 42

Chapter 5: Grounding Exercises to Protect Yourself in Social Environments and Help You Connect to Your Own Emotions 48

Chapter 6: Meditation for Empaths........................ 54

Chapter 7: Crystals and Essential Oils to Benefit Empaths 64

Chapter 8: Having Successful Relationships as an Empath 79

Chapter 9: Additional Tips for Thriving as an Empath 85

Chapter 10: Nurturing Your Inner Empath.......... 100

Conclusion 115

Introduction

The scientific world refers to empaths as 'highly-sensitive' persons, meaning that they have a greater perception of the world around them. This can cause great anxiety and make them feel exhausted and drained after dealing with large groups. For most empaths, however, the problems with social anxiety and feeling overwhelmed come from not understanding what it means to be a highly sensitive person or how to manage the symptoms.

Often, empaths do not realize what they are experiencing until later in life. They may struggle with problems like depression and anxiety as a young adult, which may be written off as puberty or natural development. However, empaths do not grow out of their sensitivity. While some learn to control it naturally or try to limit their exposure to large groups or certain people, others struggle with it until they find outside help.

If you have been struggling with problems like depression, anxiety, or an inability to function because of the strong emotions you experience, this book will give you the help you need. You will find answers for your questions about being an empath, as well as a useful questionnaire that can help you understand some of the personality traits that make you an empath. You will also learn about the science behind being an empath, as well as strategies that will help you overcome in your daily life.

This useful guide to living as an empath will help you learn how to stop simply managing your life and start living it. You will find that new opportunities are available to you, simply because you have control over the emotions you are feeling and the ability to block unwanted energies. You do not simply have to exist as an empath—you can use your gift to improve the quality of your life.

Happy reading!

Chapter 1: What Does It Mean to Be an Empath?

According to the Merriam-Webster dictionary, an empath is "one who experiences the emotions of others". This is the best way to summarize an empath's experience, as the development of their personality and who they are is affected by their ability to experience the emotions of the people around them.

Being an empath describes not only how you perceive the world around you, but the actions that you take as a result of these perceptions. For example, empaths may be more likely to cancel plans when they are feeling overwhelmed by life or they might need to find solitude somewhere during the workday. Being an empath is both a blessing and a curse that affects the way you live your life.

A Conscious Experience vs. an Empathic Experience

One of the biggest reasons that empaths struggle with understanding their experience and how to interact with the world is that their emotions do not occur consciously; they occur deep within the subconscious mind and the empath experiences the emotion before they even have a chance to consciously recognize it. The best way to explain this is to consider how you would learn how to do something simple, like throw a ball if you had never thrown one before. When a child learns to throw a ball, they first make that initial decision to learn the throwing skill. It does not matter if throwing the ball is something that could occur naturally—even someone who has great flexibility, coordination, and muscle strength would need to make the conscious decision to pick up the ball and practice before they can learn the skill.

Thinking or saying, "I want to throw that ball" creates the physical action. It creates the want that is necessary before something can be learned. Think about how difficult it would be to overcome a habit like smoking without actually wanting to do it. Even after you withdrew from the nicotine, you may still have mental cravings because you did not want to quit. Upon thinking or saying, "I want to throw that ball", it creates the physical manifestation of that action. The next step is the series of movements—picking up the ball, holding it, positioning to aim for the target, and throwing the ball. While the practice period may be shorter for a child more naturally inclined to throw the ball, that initial thought that triggers the learning process is the same. This is known as conscious learning—it is the conscious desire and process of doing something.

Consciousness is something that most people experience as they live their day-to-day lives. They are aware that they are driving to work, sitting at their desk, walking the dog, and doing the dishes. This is not to say that people do not tune out of their consciousness from time to time, but their awareness gives them a greater ability to control their experience. They have the option of tuning back in whenever they realize they have checked out of their consciousness.

Empaths experience life on a subconscious level, especially before they are aware of their condition. They have trouble blocking emotions or responding appropriately in social situations because it is their subconscious mind that experiences the other person's emotions first. This means that their thoughts, feelings, and actions have already occurred within moments and they do not have the time to slow down and consider the situation consciously. Part of learning to live as an empath is overcoming this seemingly automatic reaction to the people and places around you. You'll learn to ground yourself and consider your own emotions, as well as to block the unwanted energies you are experiencing from your encounters with other people.

Common Personality Traits of the Average Empath

Empaths exist on a spectrum, with some being more sensitive to the emotions and energies around them than others. Even though empaths have different personalities, there are some personality traits that are common among empaths, regardless of the strength of their abilities. These common traits include:

- Sensitivity to suffering- Empaths are sensitive to many pains. Some empaths can sense the

pain and suffering of animals and plants, not just humans. Empaths may feel afflicted by the same pains as the animal or may find themselves consumed by sadness. It is also common for empaths to avoid watching or reading the news, especially if it involves topics like suffering, death, or war.
- Confusion in crowds- It is almost impossible to focus when you are being berated by several emotions, whether positive, negative or a combination of both. Empaths often experience confusion or anxiety in large crowds because their mind is absorbing the emotions of everyone around them at once.
- Healing abilities- Empaths commonly affect people who are mentally, physically, or emotionally injured, simply because they put off a healing energy. When empaths absorb some of the emotions of others, it naturally releases some of the pain or stress they are feeling. Other empaths learn to project a healing, calming energy that can be beneficial to people in pain or under stress.
- Kindness- The average empaths tendency to avoid conflict and empathy for others makes them naturally kind. This kindness comes from the desire to create a more positive world, as well as the avoidance of negative emotions that come from hurting someone emotionally or physically.
- Charisma- Empaths are naturally likeable, even when they try to avoid people because of

their gift. When you fine-tune your gift, you learn to navigate work and social situations in a way that leaves people feeling that you are good-natured and charming. This charisma is something that comes naturally.
- Increased sensitivity to the environment- Empaths are sensitive in their perception of many senses, not just the energies of people. They may become anxious or irritated by certain smells, high-pitched sounds, and other nuances that most people will ignore or tune out. Additionally, loud noises, bright lights, and intense smells can become overwhelming.
- Need to pull away- It is critical for empaths to find time to themselves. Even empaths that recharge best in large crowds may find themselves seeking downtime without external stimulation. This time is critical for revisiting your own emotions and balancing your energy. Once you return to the group, you feel better able to shield yourself from the emotions of others.

How Being an Empath Affects Your Life

Though the definition of an empath offered by Merriam-Webster is accurate, it is rather brief and does little to describe the empath experience in its entirety. A much better definition is this one, published in 1759 by Adam Smith in *The Theory of Moral Sentiments*:

"Persons of delicate fibers and weak constitution of body complain, that in looking on the sores and ulcers which are exposed by beggars in the streets, they are apt to feel an itching or uneasy sensation in the corresponding part of their own bodies. The horror which they conceive at the misery of those wretches affects that particular part of them more than any other; because that horror arises from conceiving what they themselves would suffer, if they really were the wretches whom they are looking upon, and if that particular part in themselves was actually affected in the same miserable man."

This definition captures the depth of an empath's affliction and how prevalent the problems of others are in their life. If you look closely at your life, you will see the way that being an empath has changed the way that you carry out your day-to-day tasks. As you consider the way that being an empath changes your life, you are looking at the different areas of your life that you can change by controlling your gift. You will not only learn to survive in the world but will learn how to excel and how to use your empathic nature to change your life's experience.

Empaths and Relationships
One of the biggest problems that empaths have in relationships is finding the balance between spending time with their partner and having the space they need to be mentally, emotionally, and physically healthy. Empaths need to find time to recharge their energies and without doing that, it becomes a problem in serious relationships and when people are

living together, empaths have trouble finding their center. This includes romantic relationships, as well as friendships and familial relationships.

However, being an empath in a relationship also gives you greater insight into how the other person is feeling. You are better able to judge how they are feeling and why they are upset. This insight makes you a more understanding friend or partner to have. It also helps you solve problems better since you understand people's true intentions and underlying emotions.

Empaths and Social Interaction
While some empaths shy away from social interaction, especially those who have not yet learned to shield themselves, others thrive on social interaction. Part of being an empath is understanding whether you are introverted, extroverted, or a combination of both, then using that information to help you recharge after a long day of shielding yourself from the energies around you. For example, some empaths thrive around the right people. They might be recharged best by being around a small group of friends and chatting about work or going to a dog park and watching people interact with their pets. Other empaths may recharge best by taking a relaxing bath or coloring.

The key to being an empath and forming healthy social relationships is forming bonds with people who understand your needs. You should also do what you can to control your situation, such as driving yourself when you decide to go to a party, so you can leave when you are ready.

Empaths and the Workplace
Empaths in the workplace can find themselves struggling to deal with the emotions of those around them or succeeding, using their empathic abilities to navigate the workforce. Empaths may have trouble in a traditional work environment. Some thrive best when working remotely or being in charge of themselves, while others work well in healthcare, social work, animal care, and other positions where they can use their healing abilities.

When an empath plays to their strengths, they can use their abilities like conflict resolution and understanding others to help lead themselves (and the people around them) to success. Empaths have great potential for leadership if they learn to block unwanted energies and harness their empathic abilities in a positive way.

The Development of Empaths: From Childhood to Adulthood

Empaths are typically born as a highly sensitive individual, reinforcing the idea that some people are born genetically sensitive. Researcher and developmental psychologist Jerome Kagan is among the most renowned individuals to study topics like nature vs. nurture as it pertains to the psychological development of a child. Among his studies was one conducted on shyness, which started after birth. The initial study involved 462 babies of good health who were exposed to unfamiliar types of stimulation, including that of visual, auditory, and tactile natures. Approximately 20% of the babies in the test group had a highly anxious reaction to these events, indicating a much stronger response to external stimulation. Of these babies, those that were more stimulated by the cues grew into highly-sensitive, shy individuals. This happened regardless of their upbringing. Doctor Elaine Aron is also credited for her ideas on developmental psychology as they apply to highly sensitive individuals, as her research shows that there is more to empaths than the simple differences between introvertness and extrovertness as described under Jungian concepts.

Growing up as an empath comes with a unique set of struggles that must be overcome, many of which affect the child's life on a long-term scale. It is not uncommon for child empaths to cry a lot as infants, causing their parents and caretakers a great deal of frustration. They may also have more needs than the average child and if their parent does not understand these needs, they may tell their child that they need to learn to grow thicker skin or toughen up. This causes the child to lose important parts of their support system and can be the beginning of their withdrawal from social interaction because they do not believe they are tough enough for the world and they do not have their parents there to guide them through it.

Children living as empaths can also face struggles with other adults in their life. Teachers and doctors often do not realize that children are overly sensitive to their environment. Teachers may struggle with getting the child to pay attention and may report that they have trouble focusing on their lessons when the reality is that the child is over stimulated. This can cause children to be labeled incorrectly as having Attention Deficit Disorder (ADD) or Attention Deficit Hyperactive Disorder (ADHD). Parents and doctors may try to medicate the child to solve the problem, with varying degrees of success since it is not an inability to focus that is the problem. Even though the teacher, doctor, and parent cannot necessarily be blamed for this, it happens because psychologists do not necessarily understand empaths yet.

Children who live as empaths may also have trouble in households that are stressful. For example, if siblings or parents constantly fight or there is a lot of unhappiness, it can be difficult for the child to find peace. Additionally, children may not be able to find supportive friends at such a young age, since young children do not understand the importance of an empath having time to step away and regroup.

Unfortunately, most children who grow up as empaths have their problems apparent in childhood. As all these problems with socializing, school, and their home life come down on their shoulders, it is easy for children to become overwhelmed and stressed. As children grow into adolescents, they may feel as if they are a burden on the people around them or that there is something wrong with them. It is not uncommon for child empaths to develop anxiety and/or depression as a result. Though medication can help, the dosage often numbs the child to the outside world and simply covers up the problem. Even if they continuously take the medication, the numbness that they develop takes away from their connection to other people and makes friendships and relationships harder to maintain. Without medication, adolescents may try to curb or suppress their behaviors and sensitivity. By bottling everything up, the nervous system becomes overloaded and the mind gets frazzled. This results in anxiety and depression as well.

Even as an empath grows into their teenage years and becomes an adult, being an empath comes with its challenges. These are worse when they do not realize that they are highly sensitive. The key to wellness as an empath is learning to find balance between being over-stimulated and under-stimulated. While you want to engage with the outside world, so you do not become lonely or depressed, you must also find time for yourself and learn how to recharge your energy to function at work, in relationships, at home, and in your social life.

Pros and Cons of Being an Empath

Before learning to ground themselves, block unwanted energies, and cleanse the energetic space around themselves, empaths usually associate being an empath with a negative life experience. Empaths often struggle to find a place in the workplace, have difficulty maintaining intimate relationships, and may avoid social interactions because they feel exhausted at the end of a long day. Here are some of the ways that being an empath may impact your life.

Advantages

1. You heal the emotions of people around you. Even though empaths typically absorb energies, they also have the potential to manipulate the energy of a room. Simply by projecting a positive or relaxing energy outward, empaths can help calm the energy in a room. This is useful for conflict resolution and collaborating with others.

2. You have a healing energy. If you have ever listened to a relative or friend talk about their problems and felt exhausted afterward, you probably absorbed at least some of the negative emotions being described. Empaths naturally heal—which is the reason they are commonly sought out when someone close to them is having a rough time. The key to mastering this talent is to project a calming, healing energy without taking on the negative emotions yourself.

3. You can choose to seek positive energies to lift your spirits. As you can take on negative energies, you can also take on positive ones. This lets you recharge when you are feeling down. It also gives you insight into the steps you can take to make your empathic experience positive instead of negative.

4. You can connect with others on a deep level. As an empath, you have the compassion and empathy that lets you understand the world and people around you. You may be more considerate about other people's life circumstances and connect to them through this

understanding. By understanding others deeply, you can also persuade someone to see your point of view.

5. You can choose quality people to be in your life. The confusion that comes with developing relationships can be disheartening. As you learn what you need as an empath and how to control your abilities, you'll find that there are people who understand your needs as well. You can form solid connections with quality people, helping you overcome the feeling that you have to isolate to avoid feeling unwanted emotions.

Disadvantages
1. It is easy for you to become overwhelmed. Whether powerful smells, bright lights, or strong surges of emotion, empaths can easily be over-stimulated by their environment. Instead of toughing it out when your defenses are down, notice when you are feeling irritated or anxious and break away to recenter yourself.

2. You are unsure of your own emotions. Empaths often channel the emotions of people in their immediate environment, as well as the emotions of people close to them regardless of where they are. This can make it confusing when you are trying to understand how you feel about something.

3. You have difficulty finding the right social settings. You do not have to be a hobbit to be a happy empath, however, it can be hard to find the right environment. The best thing you can do is understand your unique needs and cater to them when being social.

4. You avoid confrontation. This can be a problem if someone is overstepping boundaries, being rude, or upsetting you. Instead, embrace the feelings of anger, disappointment, or sadness as they come and broach the subject. This will stop you from feeling upset in the future.

5. You do not take criticism well. Empaths often feel targeted when they are given criticism. This feels like a personal attack that can leave you feeling upset—even if you were only honked for not moving fast enough when you are sitting at a red light.

Questionnaire: Am I An Empath?

Something to be aware of as you read through this questionnaire is that your identity as an empath lies on a spectrum. Though empaths share similar parts of their life experience, such as their sensitivity to the emotions of the people around them, not every empath has the same struggles. Empaths exist on a spectrum of sensitivity, with some being more affected by emotions than others. Additionally, some empaths are naturally more adept at controlling their gift. You may not answer 'yes' to all the questions below for this reason. If you answer 'yes' to at least seven, you are an empath or highly-sensitive person.

1. Do I feel mentally exhausted after being around someone who is sad, angry, or otherwise upset?

2. Do people call me overly sensitive or say that my feelings get hurt too easily?

3. Do I need to recharge after a stressful day or experiencing negative emotions?

4. Do people say they feel better after talking to you or that you have a 'healing' nature?

5. Do you tend to attract people who need healing, whether emotionally, mentally, or physically?

6. Is it exhausting to be around people all day?

7. Am I irritated by strong smells, certain noises, or excessive talking?

8. Do I physically feel anger, sadness, happiness, anxiousness, and other emotions that reflect what my friends and the people around me are feeling?

9. Have I ever over-eaten to cope with stress?

10. Do I shy away from intimate relationships because I worry about not having my own space?

11. Do I make it a habit to drive myself if I choose to go out, so I can leave if I become overwhelmed?

12. Do I avoid watching or reading the news because it is traumatizing or physically upsetting?

13. Have I ever felt anxious, depressed, or another strong emotion for days at a time, without reason?

14. Have I ever felt a strong emotion and known to contact someone I am close with? For example, joy after a friend received good news or pain after someone was in an accident.

15. Has my energy ever changed significantly after meeting someone for the first time or feeling someone's energy when they walked in the room?

16. Have I ever felt a strong surge of emotion when walking past a group of people I don't know, like at the mall?

17. Do I feel compelled to help people who are in pain?

18. Am I intuitive about the emotions of others and what they really mean, even when their words don't match their true intentions?

By now, you should have an understanding of what it means to be an empath, both generally and what being an empath means to you. As you see where it affects the different areas of your life, you are looking at areas that you can change by learning how to control your empathic abilities.

Chapter 2: Understanding Your Empathic Nature

The ability to feel the emotions of others was once classified as a type of psychic ability, much like telekinesis, fortune-telling, and other 'powers' not explained by the scientific community. In recent decades, however, scientists have developed a deeper understanding of the brain and the way that it works. With this research came an understanding of key areas of the brain that are more sensitive in empaths. By understanding how your mind works, you can come to a greater understanding of your inherent nature as an empath.

The Mirror Neuron System

Though having empathy for a person or their situation is not the same as living as an empath, they affect the same area of the brain—the mirror neuron system. The mirror neuron system controls a person's compassion. It is made of a group of cells that reflect (or mirror) the emotions of people as the brain perceives them. In empaths or highly-sensitive people, the mirror neuron system is more sensitive. Instead of creating empathy or sympathy for that person, the brain of an empath makes them feel the emotion. This means that instead of feeling sadness for a coworker who lost her husband, you feel her sorrow as if it were your own husband that you lost.

The mirror neuron system works by subconsciously interpreting the cues of someone's emotions. This happens within a fraction of a second and you often do not realize you are taking this information in. Once the mirror neuron system perceives a certain emotion, it reflects that back and communicates it to the rest of the brain. This strong perception and response of the mirror neuron system cause you to experience that emotion.

With the average person, the mirror neuron system simply mirrors the emotion enough that it creates empathy or understanding. Things like crowd contagion (when someone gets excited because they see other concert-goers jumping around) and sympathy (a mother feeling sad when her child is in pain) are the typical response triggered by the mirror neuron system. Empaths feel these emotions on a greater level, whether the emotions are positive or negative. This lack of control in day-to-day situations is one of the reasons that new empaths feel their abilities are more of a curse than a blessing. However, strategies provided later in this book will help you learn to shield yourself from the emotions of others, cleanse yourself of negative energies, and ground yourself for control in social situations.

Other Causes of an Empathic Nature

Mirror Touch Synthesis
Mirror-touch synthesis involves an error in the way that the brain processes information. The information is input in one way, but the resulting output is a

different form. For example, synesthesia is a form of mirror-touch synthesis where the brain pairs two senses. For example, you may see colors while listening to music or taste words upon speaking or hearing them. There are several well-known figures that have synesthesia, including astronomer, mathematician, and philosopher Sir Isaac Newton, music sensation Billy Joel, and concert violinist Itzhak Perlman.

Empaths may experience mirror-touch synthesis in the way that they absorb emotions, particularly when they are not aware of what is happening. If someone is angry, empaths may feel upset or cross with others or become irritated without a cause. To overcome this, learning to be aware of your own emotions can be helpful.

Emotional Contagion
Emotional contagion happens to people in groups, whether they are empaths or not. Emotional contagion describes mobs, crowd mentality, and other phenomenon that involve people 'catching' the emotions of the people around them. For example, imagine that a like-minded group of angry people meet at a rally. They share a common dislike for whatever is making them angry. This bond makes them like the other people in the group, so when one person starts to get violent, they see it as an opportunity to get violent. Emotional contagion can also be seen in infants. Babies often cry when other babies cry. Additionally, it is not uncommon to see

newborn infants try to mimic the facial expressions of people around them.

Mimicry

Mimicry also affects the average person and not just empaths. It involves someone mirroring the actions or movements of another, whether intentionally or subconsciously. People who make direct sales are often skilled at mimicry techniques, which have been proven to increase your ability to persuade someone. People in sales often mimic a prospective customers body language and movements in a subtle way, sharing the same tone and attitude throughout the conversation. This subtle mimicry shows the person they are talking to that they are alike. As people typically 'like' themselves, they also like people who are similar to them. Surprisingly, most salesmen are so apt at this ability that the person does not realize they are being conned with the art of mimicry. Their movements are picked up by the subconscious mind, rather than the conscious mind that might detect this type of trickery. By appearing more likable and like-minded, they are better able to persuade the prospective buyer to purchase whatever they are selling.

Mimicry in Relationships

Sharing similar emotions with someone creates a likeness that draws you into them. As empaths share emotions with so many people around them, it is important that these empaths interact with people who have a positive effect on their life. A New York Times article recognized this phenomenon, drawing the conclusions that it is critical to relationship health that we learn to synchronize our moods, so they generally align with the moods of the people around us.

Imagine that your friend is going through a bad break up and she is upset. It would be considered inappropriate and rude to be happy as she is telling you her story. Instead, you must mimic her emotions, talk her through it, and then project calmer happier energy. Otherwise, your friend may think you are inconsiderate.

Even though there will be times when even the most positive people find themselves challenged in life, you should choose to be close to people who are generally positive. Learning how to center yourself and knowing when to break away and re-center are also important tools, as they will help you experience the emotions of the people around you as you choose to, rather than involuntarily.

Electrical Hypersensitivity
Electrical hypersensitivity (EHS) describes a condition where an individual has several non-specific symptoms that occur upon entering a field of high electromagnetic frequencies. The most common symptoms of EHS are vegetative symptoms that are similar to those experienced by empaths, such as fatigue, heart palpitations, difficulty concentrating, and tiredness, as well as digestive disturbances, nausea, dizziness, and dermatological symptoms including burning sensations, tingling, and redness.

Electrical hypersensitivity can make empaths sensitive to certain electromagnetic fields that vibrate at a certain frequency. An electromagnetic field describes the frequency of electromagnetic waves found around electrically charged objects. The range of the frequency depends on its strength and it affects any objects within its range. Electromagnetic charges come from the overlap of an electrical field from a stationary object and current or moving charges that make up the magnetic element.

In addition to being sensitive to certain electromagnetic frequencies, empaths may be sensitive to the electromagnetic frequencies projected by the hearts of others. Research carried out by the HeartMath Institute studied electromagnetic frequencies as they are projected from the heart, which are approximately 60 times stronger than electromagnetic waves emitted by the brain. These are rhythmic patterns that can synchronize the world around us. Empaths may be sensitive to the rhythms and frequencies of others, which explains the way they intently feel emotions. The study from the HeartMath Institute tested these frequencies using a Superconducting Quantum Interference Device (SQUID) magnometer, concluding that the frequencies of the heart may be stronger because they do not have to pass through so many layers of tissue before being emitted into the outside world.

Electromagnetic waves emit a frequency that can affect all the cells of the human body, changing the pressure of sound, blood pressure, and adjusting someone's electromagnetic field. In a way, this explains how empaths sense the changing frequencies of their loved ones when they are so far away—they simply know that something is wrong. Their sensitivity to the other person's frequency makes the empath receptive to the signals they send out, even across long distances. This works like a beacon—sending magnetic waves that travel through anything, even solid objects. As humans are constantly and unintentionally emitting these frequencies, empaths become sensitized to everyone around them. Empaths may also experience frequency changes from the electromagnetic fields of the sun, moon, and earth, as well as changes that occur when doing something like watching television or listening to music. To create a positive frequency, empaths must seek positive energy fields and stimulation.

Identifying and Accepting Yourself as an Empath

Before you can truly accept your abilities as an empath and see them for what they are, you have to accept all that you have experienced as an empath so far. Being an empath comes with its fair share of emotional trauma, particularly for people who do not realize they are a highly sensitive person because they do not have the support that they need to understand their emotions, the emotions of others, and how to handle them. Even though they may make an effort not to be as affected, it is nearly impossible to roll out of bed one morning and simply decide to be 'tougher'. It might be easy to commit to this toughness while you are still in your house, but once you are outside in the real world, it is hard once the emotions and thoughts of others start bombarding you. Even if you try to use prescribed medications or self-medicate with marijuana, alcohol, or another drug as empaths may do before they realize why they are so sensitive to the world, this just creates more problems in life.

Part of accepting your existence as an empath is understanding the emotional trauma that comes along with it, including the emotional trauma that you have already experienced. By accepting this, you began to accept yourself and your emotions as part of your history and existence. This is a necessary stage to encourage the type of healing that empaths often need to ease emotional trauma from their past. Surges of emotions can cause empaths to act out and fight with people around them or hide away where they cannot feel the emotions of others. Empaths often feel like they are going crazy, as everyday occurrences like a fight with a romantic partner or siblings, failing grades in school, the death of a loved one, disappointments and setbacks, bad presentations at work, money problems, and countless other occurrences make them feel overwhelmed by their emotions. Along with these emotions that result from their own life, empaths also experience the surge of emotions as other people go through these emotional trials. This overlap makes it hard to understand what you are feeling. For example, an empath may be perfectly content in their own relationship when they leave the house to visit their best friend. After they witness their friend getting into a fight with their significant other, however, they may return and feel unsure about their own relationship.

The problem is not this occasional experience, either. Empaths experience the emotions of people in their immediate vicinity, as well as the emotions of friends, family members, and other loved ones that they are emotionally close to. When surrounded by people, empaths experienced whichever signals are being broadcasted at the most powerful frequency. It is not uncommon for them to feel intense sadness as they walk by a coworker who buried their dog the day before and then an intense feeling of joy as another coworker learns they earned a big promotion and raise. It is not uncommon for this jumble of emotions to cause chaos. This chaos and the negative connotations that many people associate with the empathic experience make it hard to find guidance. Empaths are often diagnosed with having a mental illness, with some people even believing their ability to sense the emotions of others is a mental illness on its own. Depression, anxiety, and paranoia are among the most common mental illnesses experienced by empaths, while others are diagnosed (or misdiagnosed) with more serious illnesses like bipolar and schizophrenia because they experience frequent mood changes after drawing so many emotions in from the people around them.

If you do struggle with a diagnosed mental illness, medicate with prescription or other forms of medication, or simply struggle with the empathic experience, the first step toward recovery is accepting yourself for what you are. Instead of numbing your empathic experience or trying to block it out, accept how you have handled your empathic struggles in the past and make the commitment to improving that experience in the future. Through actively seeking wellness and following the strategies in the chapters that follow, you can improve your experience. First, however, you must realize the great impact that being an empath has on your life, including your past and present experience. Some of these strategies are going to be difficult to use at first. As with any skill, they are going to take time to develop. Remind yourself that the path to wellness is a journey and commit yourself each day to practicing grounding skills, giving yourself much-needed time alone, and understanding your own needs. By doing this, you'll find that you thrive at home, in the workplace, and in relationships.

Take a moment to consider everything that has happened in your life. Consider the way that being an empath may have influenced these events and the role that your unique nature has played in your life. Take stock of damages and successes. Now, know that you can change the outcome of these circumstances. You can change the way that you interact with others and how productive you are at work, simply by committing to understanding yourself and developing your empathic abilities instead of trying to cover them up.

Chapter 3: Blocking Unwanted Thoughts and Emotions

A major part of the empathic experience is feeling the thoughts and emotions of others. The problem is that many people in the world are experiencing negative emotions and hardships at any given time. When you are highly sensitive to your environment, it can be challenging to keep a positive mindset. This is where feelings like anxiety, depression, and fatigue come from.

The key to living as an empath is learning more about your unique skill and the toll that it can take on your body. With the right mindset, and by following the advice in this chapter, you can overcome some of the common problems that empaths face because of their sensitivity to the world around them.

Know How to Identify and Avoid Energy Vampires

One of the negative personas associated with empaths is energy vampires. Energy vampires are individuals who thrive on their ability to take or 'steal' energy from others, usually feeding off it and leaving the empath feeling drained. Usually, you feel exhausted after you encounter these types of people and it feels like they mentally, emotionally, and/or physically take something from you. They may do this by sharing an upsetting story or simply being in your presence.

Identifying Energy Vampires
It is not uncommon for empaths to be drawn to energy vampires—they may even end up in relationships with them more easily than they would other people. This happens because energy vampires are typically self-absorbed and immersed in their own existence. They do not care what is going on with the world. Empaths may be drawn to them because they pick up on their own interest in themselves, mistaking it for an interest that they share.

Energy vampires are also people who are regularly negative. They may seek attention through pessimism or believe that the world owes them more than they are receiving. Energy vampires tend to prioritize themselves, so they often complain about why life isn't fair. It is also common for energy vampires to fake their emotions, including sadness and depression. Keep in mind that this does not mean every person who is having a bad day or sharing an upsetting story is an energy vampire. It is the people who do it intentionally as a way to make you interested in their life that are energy vampires.

Another reason that empaths may be drawn to energy vampires (as most people are) is because of their charming nature. Energy vampires may come across as charming when they want to be, however, this may be deception or manipulation in disguise. They are able to pick up on other people's sensitivities and they use that to latch onto them and bring them closer. Energy vampires are also commonly overdramatic. They seek attention, so even the slightest mishaps can leave them complaining for hours. You may hear about something as trivial as spilling milk on the counter or burning a grilled cheese for hours on end.

Taking Back Your Energy
When you feel as if someone has taken your energy, it is helpful to visualize yourself getting it back. One technique you may use is to visualize a white ball of light that represents the energy you have put into that person. Imagine that white ball coming out of them and traveling back into the center of your being. You may also visualize a cord between yourself and that person, especially if you have connected yourself to them by listening to their troubles. Use a glowing sword or a pair of scissors to cut this cord, severing the connection and allowing yourself to connect to your original state.

Know When You Are Most Vulnerable

Before you learn to block unwanted emotions, you may feel as if you are vulnerable every hour of the day. This is especially true if you are in a relationship, sleep next to someone at night, or work in a field where you encounter many people on a daily basis. This discomfort with your own life might make you want to avoid social situations and limit yourself as much as possible. However, as you learn to block those things you do not want to experience, you will not feel as vulnerable all the time.

Though mastering shielding is a useful tool, it can be disconnecting with the world around you. This disconnect can become monotonous and exhausting.

Even though you may seem overwhelmed in any situation when you are not constantly shielding yourself from the world around you, if you pay close attention, you'll notice that there are some times that you feel more sensitive than others. Sensitivity can be caused by any number of things. Eating a diet with poor nutrition, not getting enough sleep, or something, like feeling inadequate at work or experiencing anxiety during a test, can cause increased sensitivity to the emotions around you. It can also be caused by being around an overwhelming amount of people.

The key to remaining positive is finding the balance between those times when you want to experience your surroundings and when you should block the emotions of others. For example, you may want to experience the overwhelming joy that fills the room if you are by a family member's bedside when they give birth. There are times when being involved emotionally in an experience can be a pleasant experience. On the other end of the spectrum, there are times when it may seem impossible to put up a shield to the outside world. Finding balance involves knowing when you are most vulnerable, so you can focus your energy when it is needed most.

Becoming aware of your interactions with people, situations, and the world around you is the first step in learning to identify those times when you are most vulnerable. Pay attention to those times when you are most sensitive. If you would like, carry around a notebook and mark down some of the major experiences during the day, especially when you are feeling vulnerable to the emotions around you. Jot down what was happening at the time, the people you were interacting with, the time of day/night, and your surroundings. Then, assign them a number between one and ten, with one being a situation where you felt comfortable and not vulnerable and ten being any time you feel extremely vulnerable.

As you revisit these scenarios later, think about the root causes. Was there a specific person present that you felt especially sensitive to their emotions? What do you think caused this sensitivity? Were you worried about how they would see you or do you feel intimidated? Are you unsure of how you should act when they are nearby? When considering situations, think about the underlying factors that might be triggering your negative emotions. Did you not get enough sleep the night before and are having a hard time blocking? Are you overwhelmed by the number of people nearby? As you collect more information, you'll find that there are times when you have heightened sensitivity to the world around you.

Identify Negative Sources of Energy

The average empath's caring nature makes it difficult for them to identify negative sources of energy in their life. They may not realize that they are experiencing negative energies because they always feel drained after confrontations. However, not every encounter in your life should be exhausting. There are people who have positive, uplifting energies.

Keep in mind that not everyone will be positive all the time. When you care about someone, there may be times when they are upset and choose to be around them. The people that you should avoid do not experience upset occasionally—every encounter with them is exhausting. For example, empaths often feel exhausted after being around narcissists, who are commonly controlling and over-critical of the people around them.

By eliminating the negative people in your life, you automatically invite better, more positive experiences. The easiest way to identify someone with a negative persona is to think about the focus of the conversation when someone is around. Do they take the time to ask you how you are doing or listen to your problems, or does the conversation focus primarily on their life? Do they ever make you feel like you are inadequate, by criticizing your actions or behaviors? People who act in this way often have ill intentions and the relationship that they form with you will never be a healthy one. Once you have identified someone as being negative, you should limit your exposure to them. This is not always possible. For example, there may be one member of your family that you cannot exclude from your life without avoiding family get-togethers or you may have a coworker that is especially difficult.

Something that empaths have to overcome as they start to weed people out of their lives is the struggles they face after 'abandoning' someone. It is hard to put distance between yourself and others when you are an empath, because you may feel guilty or as if you are ostracizing them. Keep in mind that it is possible to remain respectful without allowing that person to continue to negatively affect your energy. Additionally, if they are an emotional vampire, narcissist, or generally negative, it won't be long before they replace you with someone else that will let them feed off their energy.

Create a Set of Values for Yourself

As empaths are heavily influenced by emotions, it can be difficult to hold true to your values once someone reacts to you standing your ground. For example, empaths typically should take time to cleanse themselves of bad energies before bedtime, so they do not have to carry those negative energies with them all night, disrupting their sleep patterns. Imagine for a moment that you have a routine you follow every night before bed. You receive an invitation to a dinner party around this time, though, or a coworker asked you to finish their part of a project. You may feel obligated to help with these things, but it is important to dedicate time to yourself. Empaths may not want to reject what others ask of them, but sometimes it becomes necessary to maintain your inner peace.

To be healthy as an empath, you have to set ground rules for what you are willing to compromise on and what you are not. Maintaining your mental and emotional health must be your top priority. There are times when you might sacrifice the things you need to help someone you care about. However, it is critical that you know what you need to function in day-to-day society.

As you set values, learn to stick to them. You should not feel obligated to remain in situations that do not promote your wellness. Instead, learn to walk away. It should not matter who is involved—if something does not promote your well-being, walk away. Some examples of things you may not compromise on include going to work when you are stressed (but not feeling obligated to take on extra work when someone else is slacking) or spending quality time with your family several times a week (but knowing that you have to commit time to yourself as well). It may be best to write these things down; creating a list will keep you focused on living a life that does not compromise your values.

Break Away When Needed

When you are feeling overwhelmed by negative energies, before you can refocus yourself, you may need to break away. It will be almost impossible to ground yourself once you are overwhelmed if you are still surrounded by the situation that overwhelmed you. This retreat can be as simple as stepping away to the bathroom, finding an empty room, or going outside for some fresh air. Then, you can use an exercise to cleanse yourself of negative energies, then ground yourself and refresh your shield.

Invite Positivity into Your Life

Part of having a better experience as an empath is learning to take control by inviting positivity into your life. The science of having a positive mindset shows that people who are optimistic or have a positive attitude are generally happier. This is because they encourage positive experiences and tend to see things in the light of why they are 'good', rather than what is wrong with the situation.

Something that you can do to keep yourself in a positive mindset is to carry around something that is important to you and brings you joy. This could be a photo of your partner or child, a family member, or a pet. Think about the warmth and joy that you experience when in that person's presence. As you do this, consider some of the traits that you love the most about them. Find someone in your immediate area and notice these traits in them, either because they are true traits or by visualizing them. As you survey your environment, take note of the positive ones and overlook the negative ones. By consciously willing yourself to have a positive experience, you will find that the way you interact with the world becomes better.

Another way to invite positivity into your life is to find time to do the things you love. It is not uncommon for empaths to get in the habit of putting their needs to the side when someone calls them and asks to talk or needs help moving. When you get in the habit of always doing something for someone else, however, it is easy to forget that you should be a priority too. Doing something you love is as easy as sitting down and coloring for an hour, immersing yourself in a book, riding your motorcycle, going for a hike, or doing anything else that you love. If you are guilty of being 'too busy' to find time for yourself, write at least 20 minutes on days that you work and one hour on days that you do not work to do something for yourself. Be sure that you thoroughly enjoy the experience. Don't just stare blankly at the television or stare at the ground while you walk through the woods—fully immerse yourself in the experience and be sure that you are having a good time while doing it. By making time for the things that make you happy, positivity and happiness will become priorities in your life. As this happens, the more positive benefits and experiences associated with being an empath will fall into place naturally.

Learn How to Shield Yourself from Unwanted Energies

A good strategy when dealing with energy vampires or unwanted energies is to practice shielding. Shielding is a technique that allows you to stop the negative energies of others from permeating your shield, which is a bubble of protective energy that you put up around yourself. The best shielding techniques are those used with visualization since you can imagine a physical shield around your body and stop yourself from feeling anything past that point.

It is important to note that before you shield yourself from negative energies, you must first be sure that the negative experience you are having is not some feeling that is hanging around you. If you do not know how to cleanse yourself yet, use one of the strategies provided in the chapter that follows. Once you are cleansed of negative energies that may exist within your shield area, use the following strategy to put yourself in a bubble.

Take several deep breaths. Once you are at peace, focus on grounding yourself and becoming immersed in your self-awareness. Then, imagine the self-awareness growing until it begins a film that pushes past your skin. Continue to project this film outward as if it were a bubble, focusing on your self-awareness and your presence inside of this cleansed bubble. This aura will protect you from the emotions of others as you go through your day.

Chapter 4: Cleansing Yourself of Unwanted Energies

Even once empaths learn to shield themselves from negative energies, there are still going to be some situations that will be overwhelming. This might happen after not getting enough sleep before work or being obligated to be around a large group of people. Negative experiences will still happen. However, you can stop feeling bad by learning to cleanse yourself of these negative energies. The strategies in this chapter will teach you how to stop negativity from clouding your thoughts, feelings, and emotions. Generally, you should use a grounding exercise (discussed in the next chapter) to help you find your center of balance after you have neutralized the negative energies.

Why You Need to Cleanse Yourself of Negative Energies

As an empath, the things that you come into contact with through the day can latch on and hold fast, making it hard to shake negative energies. Even if you had an unpleasant interaction with your coworker in the morning, for example, it can hang around with you all day. If you do not cleanse yourself before bed, it may continue to cling to you until work the next morning. As you gather more negative energies throughout the day, you will find yourself increasingly overwhelmed and more sensitive to the world around you. This can cause feelings of sadness, anxiety, anger, and other unpleasant feelings that you cannot seem to shake.

Cleansing is for those times when you need to cleanse yourself of negative energies and restore balance to your body. Some strategies, like those centered on visualization, can be used anywhere. Others might require a few tools. For additional tips on cleansing your area of negative energies, check out the chapter on crystals and essential oils later in the book.

Strategy #1: Visualizations to Remove Unwanted Energies

The major benefit of visualization techniques is that they can be done almost anywhere. As long as you can find a quiet area where you can focus, visualization can be done without any tool but your mind. Here are a few strategies you can use:

- Take several deep breaths, with the intent of quieting your mind. Once you are relaxed, picture a gray mist or dark cloud as it rises from your body. As this mist continues to rise, you feel the negativity being lifted. The clouds will lift and clear. As they clear, your mind will follow.
- Breathe deeply as you imagine all the negative energies being gathered in bubbles. Visualize bubbles floating from your mouth and nostrils as you exhale, being released into the air and floating away. You should feel lighter after this exercise, as your mind is no longer heavy with negative experiences.

Strategy #2: Washing Away Negative Energies

When you have had a particularly long day or encountered someone giving off negative emotions, you may not always be able to effectively block the energies of others. This visualization technique is useful for releasing those energies that tend to stick around after you have been worn down.

This technique can be used in two different ways. The most convenient is to wash your hands under running water, making an effort to visualize the negative energies flowing from your heart and mind, traveling down your arms and wrists, and finally being washed from your hands. Visualize that all these negative feelings are going down the drain and continue to wash until you feel lighter, like the physical weight of the energies has been lifted and the emotions you are experiencing no longer hold.

The second method works best just before bed or after a particularly long day. Like with washing your hands, you are going to visualize the energies being brought to the surface of your skin and being washed away from your body. These energies are going to run with the water down the drain, releasing you of any negative or toxic emotions that might linger. When you step out of the shower, you will feel considerably lighter and more centered on yourself. By rinsing away residual energies, you are grounding yourself to your own emotions. While this technique can be used any time that you can take a shower, it works especially well before bedtime. As you will not be venturing back outside before your shower, it is perfect to give yourself a full night of rest. You will find you wake up refreshed and ready to tackle the day.

Strategy #3: Using Sage

One of the most powerful cleansing techniques has been passed down through Native American culture for centuries. Smudging involves using sage to cleanse areas of energy. To perform a smudging ceremony, dried sage leaves are tied together tight enough that they are bound securely. Then, the sage is burned. This is believed to work because of the powerful energy of sage, which permeates the air in the room. As you smudge, it is important to state your intention. For example, you may smudge around the air you are breathing and state that you are trying to cleanse the air and yourself of negative energies.

Another way to use sage is in a bath. As the oils and warm water permeate the skin, it absorbs and offers a deep cleaning experience. Generally, 5-10 drops of sage oil will do. If you would like, you can add additional grounding or cleansing oils to the bath to increase the effects. While you can take a sage bath any time, it is especially beneficial at night when you can remain cleansed as you sleep. This will give you a deep, rejuvenating night of sleep.

Strategy #4: Acupuncture

Acupuncture is a strategy commonly used in Traditional Chinese Medicine practices. Traditional Chinese Medicine focuses on the body as a whole, which is why acupuncture is commonly used to promote total-body wellness. Acupuncture is typically used to align the flow of energy through your body. As your energies are focused, anything that you are holding onto or emotions that you have repressed will be released. You will also feel the return of new, positive energies that flow through you.

Some people are nervous when they try acupuncture for the first time, as the practice involves using long, thin needles that are inserted at key points of the body. Acupuncture is not generally painful, as the needles are very thin, and a licensed acupuncturist knows where to insert the needles, so they do not hurt. If you do choose this method to relieve tension and help balance the flow of energy through your body, be sure to choose an acupuncturist that is licensed to practice. You should also choose a facility that properly sterilizes equipment between sessions.

Strategy #5: Chakra Balancing

Even though the root chakra and throat chakra are considered the most important for empaths, full-body chakra balancing can help you cleanse yourself of unwanted energies. When you realign your chakras, it encourages a balance. As all the energies that do not belong to you flow from your body and your chakras become aligned, it helps you find your inner self.

There are several ways that you can balance your chakras. One practice is Reiki, which is commonly practiced under a professional until you become skilled at it. You can also balance your chakras through meditative practice. You can work with a coach, attend a yoga or meditation class that focuses specifically on helping you achieve balance of your chakras, or look for videos or guided meditation scripts online.

Chapter 5: Grounding Exercises to Protect Yourself in Social Environments and Help You Connect to Your Own Emotions

One of the biggest struggles of an empath is going out in public, whether to their workplace, social gatherings, or even the grocery store. Grounding strategies describe techniques that you can use to ground, or center, yourself. This centering is intended to draw your focus inward, giving you an opportunity to assess how you are feeling and separate yourself from the people around you. As you fine-tune your grounding abilities, you'll find yourself more energized in social settings than you were before. Additionally, you'll find yourself better able to protect yourself from the energy being projected by people around you, giving you greater control over your emotions and the way that you experience life.

In addition to increasing your control, learning grounding strategies will help you find a sense of balance in your life. Achieving balance as an empath is about learning when to ground yourself and when to leave yourself emotionally sensitive. For example, you may want to ground yourself when talking to a coworker who always gossips and says negative things about someone, but you may want to be in tune with your emotions when speaking to a friend who is going through a rough time in their life.

As you find balance, you will also be more confident in getting the things you need in life. Communication channels will open up and you will be able to express your own emotions, without the emotions of others getting in the way. You will also find that you are not as emotionally burnt out at the end of the average day. Keep in mind as you read the following chapter that it may feel unnatural to ground yourself at first. Most empaths have gone through their entire lives experiencing the emotions of others and without that outside influence, they do not feel like their 'normal' selves. Once this initial discomfort or unnaturalness passes, you'll start experiencing the benefits of grounding yourself.

Strategy #1: Rooting Yourself

Visualization is one of the most beneficial tools for people who are learning to control their empathic nature, as it gives you something solid to focus on. For some people, it is easier than mediation and other techniques that rely on your ability to focus on nothingness. To practice this strategy, you are going to visualize yourself as a tree. Your body makes up the trunk and your head and arms the branches. You can put them over your head if it makes visualization either. From your feet, you are going to visualize roots growing and holding you fast to the earth. These roots represent the core of your being. When you reflect on yourself as a tree, you find yourself grounded to where you stand and grounded to your own emotions, rather than letting yourself float away in the thoughts and emotions of others.

You can visualize yourself as a tree wherever you are. The roots are not permanent, they are flexible and will follow you as you move your feet, keeping the core of your being grounded regardless of where you go. This leaves you deeply rooted within the core of yourself, attached to your own feelings and emotions.

Strategy #2: Mindful Eating

Mindful eating is something that you can do at meal times (so you don't have to avoid nice dates at restaurants or the cafeteria at lunch), as well as a tool you can use when you are feeling overwhelmed. The best foods to do mindful eating with are those that have texture or variety. For example, you might carry trail mix with you or pack a sandwich or pasta dish that has several ingredients.

To eat mindfully, you need to take small bites. Remember that you are not eating out of compulsion or with the intent of getting full, but to instead give yourself a place to focus your attention. Chew your food slowly, giving it time to move around in your mouth and interact with different taste buds. Pay attention to the textures and flavors that come together with each bite. A raisin is going to be sweet and sticky, while an almond has a slightly sweet taste and crunchy exterior.

This grounding technique can be useful in a lot of settings, as it is easy to carry a small handful of trail mix or some gummies in your pocket. It is also useful when you are having lunch with someone or out on a date since you will not be distracted by the other person's jitteriness or the anger of the woman at the table next to you when she catches her husband giving the waitress a once-over.

Strategy #3: Deep Reflection

One of the reasons that empaths feel disconnected from their own experience is because they don't take the time to deeply reflect on their own emotions. It is easy to want to tune out everything after a long day, even yourself. It is easy to neglect your own emotions, especially when you have spent the day being bombarded with everyone else's. Reflection helps you handle your own issues, by giving you the opportunity to question your life circumstances and how you are feeling about them. This is critical for success in life, especially in situations where you may need to make changes or a decision. Reflection is as simple as finding a quiet space in your home or going somewhere you can be alone in nature and asking yourself some questions.

It can be helpful to meditate for a few moments before this exercise or to use one of the other grounding techniques in this chapter to help you connect to your own flow of energy. Once you feel in tune with yourself, ask questions like:

- What is happening in my life right now?
- Is there anything happening that might trigger negative feelings?
- What specific emotions am I experiencing as I think about my life?
- Are the negative emotions I am experiencing mine or do they belong to another person or group of people?
- When was I last around people where I felt negatively?
- Are the emotions I am feeling positive? Do they serve my purpose?
- Which emotions should I own? Which of these should I release?

Once you understand which emotions are your own and which you should release, use one of the techniques in the previous chapter to cleanse yourself of the energies you no longer want to experience.

Strategy #4: Enjoy Physical Connections to the Earth

When you touch grass, sand, dirt, concrete, water, and other elements of the earth, you are fostering a deeper connection to the earth. This physical connection creates a bond both physically and mentally, making it easier to return to this state and ground yourself when you need to. Connecting to the earth can also benefit your health. Touching it with your bare feet, hands, or body allows you to absorb electrons from the earth. These electrons function as antioxidants to fight free radicals in the body. Free radicals typically attack healthy cells, such in the cases of autoimmune diseases and cancer, for example. This helps sustain your health.

Using Nature to Connect to Your True Self
In addition to just physically touching the earth, visiting different nature spots can be very healing. Weather permitting, take off your shoes and walk alongside the lakeshore, over a soft, mossy clearing in the woods, or through a grassy, flower-filled hill at your local dog park. Make an effort to clear your mind and feel the energy of the earth flow through you. Use the tree visualization mentioned earlier in this chapter to deepen this connection if you are having trouble. Once you feel the vibrations from that connection, reflect on how it makes you feel inside. If you are going through anything in life, reflect on that situation and how it might make you feel. Consciously accept those emotions that belong to you and release those that do not. If you are alone, feel free to speak out loud to yourself and analyze your thought process. This will help you connect to your true self.

Once you have created this connection, feel all the negative energies and those thoughts that do not serve your true self travel through your feet and into the earth. As these disperse, imagine that there is a green energy flowing up through the earth and in through your feet. This energy is renewing and positive, filling you with a healing, vibrating energy.

Chapter 6: Meditation for Empaths

Meditation is beneficial for the average person. It is a time set aside where the mind can be calm and quiet, something that is much different than the hustle-and-bustle that most people experience during the day. Meditation has a host of benefits for your mental and physical health. As calmness comes over you, you will find yourself feeling refreshed. This can recharge your mental energies when you are having trouble shielding yourself from the outside world and leaves you a blank slate ready to take on newer, more positive energies.

How to Meditate

There are many forms of meditation, each of them with a specific goal or focus. Each of them is a practice that trains the mind in a way, generally focusing on creating a state of calm or inducing a specific feeling. This section will provide a basic overview of meditation. Later in the chapter, you will find a script that you can use for guided meditation, which will be explained in the next section.

Step 1: Get Comfortable
Being comfortable is an important part of meditation, as you cannot focus on clearing your mind if your posture is hurting your spine or your clothing is making you itchy. Be sure you are wearing comfortable clothes and find somewhere to sit or lie

down. You can sit on the floor with your legs crossed, on a chair with your legs hanging down, or lie down completely. Sit with your back tall if you are sitting, but do not be rigid. You should also be sure you choose the right environment for meditation—you will not be successful in a loud room. Choose somewhere that is quiet and distraction-free.

Step 2: Close Your Eyes
Once you are ready, close your eyes. Breathe normally for a few moments and note how your body feels before you move onto the next step.

Step 3: Focus on Your Breaths
Now, begin to breathe consciously. Inhale for a count of 3, exhale for a count of 3. Eventually, stop counting and allow your breathing to continue. If it makes it easier, think 'in' and 'out' with each breath. Pay attention to the way that each inhale fills your abdomen and chest. Then, notice how it deflates with each exhale. Continue to focus on your breaths until you are thinking of nothing else.

Step 4: Clear Your Mind
Once your mind is cleared, you may continue to breathe and meditate as long as you would like. If you find yourself becoming unfocused, do not become critical or harsh. Instead, acknowledge that you had a thought or that your mind is wandering and let it pass through you and into the air with your next inhale. Focus again on your breaths and the way that your body inflates and deflates each time.

Guided Meditation

Guided meditation is an excellent choice for empaths who may struggle to clear their mind, whether they are new to meditation or overwhelmed by the emotions they are feeling. Guided meditation is a good alternative because rather than trying to clear your mind, a voice helps you through the meditation exercise and keeps you focused. You can find audio recordings of guided meditation online or create your own by recording your voice speaking a meditation.

There are guided meditations for a wide variety of purpose. Two that benefit empaths the most are guided meditation for grounding and guided meditation to release negative energies. Below, you'll find an explanation for what to look for in these types of recordings, as well as a sample script that you can use to create your own guided meditation.

Guided meditation that has been designed to encourage grounding usually focuses on the root chakra. As you breathe your energy downward into the earth, you should feel a connection and your breathing should slow. This helps balance you. As you find this balance, you will also find that the negative energies are released from your body. This type of meditation should also bring about clarity.

Sample Guided Meditation Script
As you begin, you should be sitting comfortably with your spine elongated.

Take a deep breath in...

And slowly release it.

Take another deep breath in...

And slowly release it.

Take a third deep breath, paying attention to how it fills your chest and abdomen...

Now, feel your chest and abdomen become soft as you slowly push the air out.

Continue to breathe, deeply inhaling and exhaling to fill and deflate with each breath...

In...

Out...

In...

Out...

Now, be sure that your eyes are closed and turn your focus to the different areas of your body, starting with your head.

Mentally scan each area of your body and note any tension you may feel...

The head...

The neck and shoulders...

Down the arms and fingers...

As you find areas of tension, squeeze the muscles tighter and then release...

Squeeze...

And release...

Continue to do this with each area of your body that feels tense,

Noticing how each area feels relaxed after you release.

In the chest and abdomen...

Through your back, pelvic area, and hips...

Down your thighs and knees...

To your calves, ankles, feet, and toes.

As you finish,

Your entire body should be in a state of relaxation.

Now, bring all your attention to the root chakra...

Feeling the energy pool near the base of your spine...

This is the center of your energy and life force,

Your connection to the earth.

If you are interrupted by any thoughts, release them...

Release distractions from your mind until your only focus is your root chakra.

Now, visualize a red, glowing ball of energy at your root chakra...

With each breath, this ball becomes brighter.

As the power of the ball increases, the ball of energy starts to spin with a counterclockwise motion....

As it spins faster and faster, turn your attention back to your breaths.

With each exhale, feel any energies that do not align with your root chakra release...

Consciously identify those things that are harming your root chakra and your ability to find peace.

Then, set the intention to release these energies as they occur...

Making it habit to release them as they occur in your daily activities.

Continue this process...

Taking deep breaths in and out...

Breathe in red light as that ball of energy continues to glow bright,

Breathe out those things that do not serve you.

Now, you are going to balance the root chakra by assuming Guyon mudra...

A hand position that helps balance the root chakra...

Join your thumb and index finger in a circular position,

Allowing your other fingers to sit loosely and relaxed away from the hand.

Continue to hold this position and relax your body...

Breathing in and out for several breaths...

In...

Out...

In...

Out...

In...

Out...

Continue to sit as long as you would like, until you feel centered and at one with yourself...

You should feel balanced and relaxed...

You should feel clear...

You should feel as if the weight of negative energies in your life has been lifted...

Now, affirm your centeredness and groundedness by speaking aloud...

I am grounded.

I am physically aware and comfortable in my surroundings.

I feel my connection to all living things, as well as the earth below me.

My body is full of vitality and energy.

My connection to the earth feels effortless.

I feel secure and safe in my environment.

I thrive from my relationship with the all that is around me.

My passion for life burns strongly.

I listen to the messages of my body and my inner self.

I allow my creative force to inspire my motivation and accomplish my goals.

I respect myself and trust my ability to know when I need to be replenished.

I am in tune with my body and have a healthy relationship with money.

I connect my soul with my physical body through the movements of dance and exercise.

Reflect now on which of these statements resonated with you.

Try to repeat those that did not, giving yourself a moment to feel the energy as the truth resonates within you.

Fully connect with these truths and all that you want to be.

Now, imagine that the earth is glowing bright red as it quakes beneath you...

As the earth quakes, you feel the rumble at the base of your spine...

The longer you focus, the more the intensity of the quaking grows...

The quaking travels from your spine to your abdomen, radiating upward as it fills your body and vibrates through your legs and chest.

Finally, the quaking reaches your back, arms, neck, and head.

As the ground continues to quake your entire being,

It shakes all the energy loose that does not belong to you...

As well as that energy that does not serve your higher purpose...

Negative beliefs shake through the cracks of the ground around you...

As the quake shakes this free, your breaths allow positive, bright, and lively energies to flow in through your root chakra...

This bright, red energy flows through your spine from the earth...

The healing vibrations fill you with passion and life...

Now, began to recite a deep chant,

'Ohm' will work fine...

You are going to chant three times, each time allowing the vibrations from the chant to resonate through your whole body and every fiber of your being...

Ohm…

Ohm…

Ohm…

Now, continue to breathe, imagining that your red root energy is returning to your base…

Continue to breathe and relax until you are ready to return to a conscious awareness of your surroundings.

Chapter 7: Crystals and Essential Oils to Benefit Empaths

Things that are of the earth often deepen a connection to the earth, helping with grounding and producing other effects. Something, like having a crystal in your proximity or using essential oils for aromatherapy, can be grounding, cleanse you of negative energies, help with shielding, and more. This chapter will go over some of the ways that you can use crystals and essential oils to help channel, block, and improve the energies in your life, as well as which crystals and oils are the best choices for your desired outcome.

Crystals

Among the many ways that empaths are affected by the world around them is the influence of vibrational frequencies. Crystals are solid objects formed by molecules of the earth bonding together, usually over the course of millions of years. As the crystals undergo physical changes caused by pressure and high temperatures, the resulting energies are stored within. The stored energies then travel through the molecules that make up the crystal and project a specific and unique frequency.

How to Use Crystals
One of the great things about crystals is that simply by being in their presence, you can experience some of the benefits. Many empaths choose to wear crystal

jewelry, as this allows their crystal to always be with them. Another option is to carry a crystal around with you—people often choose smooth stones for this, so they can rub them when they are anxious or depressed. Another option is to set it on your desk or next to your bed—simply being within the range of the crystal will help you synchronize your own energies with the frequency of the crystal you have chosen.

Caring for Crystals
The way that crystals attract and hold energies makes them susceptible to picking up negative energies, especially heavy stones that absorb energy like hematite. When you first bring a crystal home, you should cleanse it and recharge it. Most crystals can be cleansed in a salt bath. Put 1-2 tablespoons of salt into lukewarm water and place the crystal inside. Let it soak at least 24 hours. If you have a crystal that is soft or metallic in nature, it may dissipate or become rusted if you place it in salt water. Some crystals that should not be soaked in a salt bath include lodestone, hematite, calcite, turquoise, mica, malachite, pyrite, lepidolite, and selenite. In this case, you can use selenite to cleanse the crystal.

To use selenite for cleansing your crystal, set the crystals you wish to clean with a piece of selenite. Let these crystals sit together overnight. The selenite will draw out any negative energies. Another alternative is burying the crystals in dry Himalayan salt to cleanse them.

When you charge your crystals, you are returning their natural healing properties to them. The best way to charge crystals is in the moonlight, especially a full moon. Choose a clear night to charge your crystals and place them on a windowsill or outside, where they will receive direct moonlight through the night.

Crystals that Benefit Empaths

Some crystals will help ground you to the energy of the earth, giving you the ability to connect to its energy. This lets you tune into your own energy and experience while shielding your mind and body from the emotions of others. Other crystals may work to promote cleansing of negative energies or promote a positive mood or mindset. Here is a list of some of the best crystals for empaths and what they do.

- Prasiolite- This stone both grounds you to the inner energy of the earth and removes negative energies that may exist within your mind, body, and space. The flow of energy through your body works as an exchange. As the negative energy flows out, positive energies replace it. This leaves you feeling centered and replenished.
- Bloodstone- Bloodstones work with the natural grid of the earth to encourage grounding and stability. It works by grounding you to your conscious experience and making you aware in the present moment. Bloodstone also interacts with the heart, promoting courage and strength.
- Hematite- The hematite crystal has a magnetic energy that interacts with the metallic elements of the earth to ground you. This

grounding energy centers you through this connection to the earth and it encourages balance and calmness. Hematite stones also draw out negative energy and absorbing it as its own. It is a good choice for some empaths, but others find that the stone is too heavy or too powerful for them to carry.

- Shungite Stone- This is known as the most powerful crystal for bringing a state of balance to the root chakra. Shungite encourages a state of mind where you deal with toxic mental issues, emotions, and other things that do not serve your benefit. It helps you understand these issues, so you may move past them. By benefiting the root chakra, shungite creates a solid foundation that other chakras can become balanced upon and encourages overall wellness.
- Carnelian- Carnelian stones that are either deep orange or red are grounding in nature. They also provide a sense of comfort while boosting your confidence, which can be helpful in the workplace or social situations. Something to note is that it is common for 'carnelian' jewelry to be simulated by dying agate. Be sure you have the authentic stone to get the full benefits.
- Purple Jade- This crystal is ideal for protecting empaths. One of the ways that it works is by giving you greater insight into your own emotions, helping you block and reject those that do not belong to you. Purple jade also

connects you to the earth star chakra. This chakra exists even deeper than the root chakra, positioned about 6 inches below your feet within the earth. This offers a deep grounding experience.
- Black Tourmaline- Black tourmaline is a good choice for empaths who work as healers. It dispels negative energy, so you do not absorb it. The black tourmaline works to protect and shield you, whether from a single person or your whole environment.
- Boji Stones- If you are feeling 'spacey' or out of touch, this crystal invites balance into your life. These spacey feelings are often caused by being out of touch with your physical body. Boji stones work by cleansing your aura and restoring your groundedness.
- Lepidolite- This crystal is known for its ability to enhance the abilities of any other crystal. It also reduces anxiety that is a common symptom for empaths. Its ability to promote peace can also help you find comfort in your relationships and improve your ability to sleep.
- Obsidian- Obsidian creates a deep connection to the earth, helping you become grounded and experience stability. It is known for its protective nature, helping you remove negative energy from your immediate environment. It is also known for channeling dark energy and releasing it into the light.

- Smoky Quartz- The smoky quartz crystal benefits the root chakra, which is the center of all the body's chakras and connects you to the earth. Smoky quartz works by neutralizing negative energies and vibrations, drawing light in as they are removed.
- Magnetite- The magnetic properties of metallic magnetite lets it attract the natural elements of the earth. This has a deep grounding effect. It can also help align your energies, creating a state of balance that is important for connecting to your inner self.
- Jasper- Jasper crystals come in several patterns and colors. Traditionally, the stone that works best will be the one that is most attractive to you, as jasper crystals are known for their ability to call to the people who need them. Jasper works by creating a deep connection to the earth. The color and pattern of the crystal you choose also affects how it works. For example, the popular red jasper stone returns energy to your body.
- Amethyst- Amethyst is known for increasing an empath's intuition. This is important when you are trying to enhance your empathic abilities or trying to gain a greater sense of what you need to be mentally and emotionally healthy. Greater intuition can also help you identify which emotions are yours and which belong to other people.
- Fire Agate- Though this is not a popular crystal, it works well for some empaths because of its deep connection to the chakra

system. It helps energies flow through the chakras and is grounding in nature. In addition to creating a powerful connection to the earth, fire agate helps you overcome obstacles, blockages, and negative energies, encouraging a renewed energy and inviting change into your life.

- Malachite- This stone helps remove emotional blockages that empaths commonly experience after being under extreme stress. It absorbs negative emotions, especially those that have rooted deep inside your being.
- K2 Stone- This crystal is created through a fusion of celestial azurite and grounding granite. It helps you understand and encourage the connection between the universe and its life energy and your earthly experiences. It can help you find the balance you need between intuition and meeting earthly demands.
- Red Calcite- When you are feeling out of touch with your consciousness, this crystal works to promote feelings of calm and groundedness. It also helps bring about a state of focus, relieving the feelings of being detached from your current experience.
- Rose Quartz- This crystal interacts with the heart, promoting feelings of grounding and unconditional love. This can be beneficial for empaths trying to find security or balance in relationships. It also works to push away negative emotions you may be experiencing.

Essential Oils

Essential oils describe any blend of plant parts, including the leaves, flowers, stems, seeds, and roots. As essential oils are of the earth, much like crystals, they possess unique grounding abilities that help you strengthen your connection to the earth. They also have unique properties based on the plant they are made from.

How to Use Essential Oils
Essential oils can be used in several different ways, which can create different effects. Some can be added to lotion, oils, or other beauty products and rubbed directly into your skin. Others can be diffused or added to water and sprayed in the air, resulting in an aromatherapy experience that encourages grounding and healing. If you do choose to buy essential oils, be sure they are 100% pure to get the full effects.

When you are applying oils to your skin, you should add it to a carrier oil like shea butter, coconut oil, grapeseed oil, sweet almond oil, and jojoba oil. You can also add them to witch hazel or water and use it as a spritzer, either in the air or on your skin. Since some oils break down plastics, they should be stored in glass bottles or jars.

Before you start using an essential oil, you should do research on it. Something to remember is that just because something is considered natural, it does not mean that it is non-toxic. For example, citrus oils like lemon oils can have the side effect of photosensitivity, especially when applied directly to the skin. This means that you are more likely to experience sunburn. Additionally, oils like tea tree oil have a wide range of benefits—but they are also toxic when ingested. Doing research beforehand will keep you experiencing the benefits of essential oils without putting yourself at risk of side effects. You should also seek advice if you take medications to be sure there will not be negative interactions.

Essential Oils That Benefit Empaths
Generally, any pure essential oil or blend of essential oils can be beneficial for empaths. There are some, however, that contain ingredients known as sesquiterpenes. These large, heavy molecules make a great base fragrance and usually have deep, resinous aromas. Here are some of the best essential oils to encourage grounding, relaxation, connectedness, and other benefits for empaths.

- Basil- If you work somewhere that you may be physically drained by people you encounter through the day, basil oil is a good option. Basil is energizing and uplifting because of the way it works on the nerves. It is also said to keep away negative energies and spirits. To use basil oil, apply a diluted solution to your feet and chest after waking up in the morning. Some other benefits of basil include its benefits for lifting depression, anxiety, and fatigue, which are common problems that empaths may deal with.

- Cypress- Cypress is herbaceous in nature. It is known for its shielding abilities and can help bring about a sense of security.
- Black Spruce- Black spruce oil is one of the best choices for empaths because of its many benefits. It encourages emotional healing and balances moods, allowing someone who is depressed to be uplifted and someone who is anxious to become calm. Black spruce also supports the endocrine system and is known for its clarifying properties. Its ability to purify has made it a major element of some Native American rituals.
- Chamomile- When you are trying to relax at night, chamomile is a good option. It is anti-inflammatory and sedative. When you use it for relaxation and cleanse yourself before bed, it can encourage a deep, rejuvenating sleep that leaves you with the mental strength you need to fight off negative energies the next day.
- Patchouli- Patchouli is especially beneficial for empaths who take on the physical ailments of the people around them. It can also be useful for people who work in the healthcare field. It works by grounding you to your own body, allowing you to connect to your inner being instead of taking on the energies and symptoms put out by other people.
- Nutmeg- This oil has a warm, spicy aroma that is perfect for promoting energy when you are feeling overwhelmed or intimidated by the day

ahead. It is also comforting because of its familiarity and uplifting.
- Rosemary- Rosemary has a woodsy, familiar scent. It is known for uplifting moods and promoting mental clarity.
- Geranium- Geranium is beneficial for empaths because it helps create balance, by working to lift depressive moods and sedate anxiety. This makes it perfect for use after being around large groups of people and when you are experiencing a wide variety of conflicting emotions.
- Clove- Clove is beneficial for empaths who are easily influenced by the energies and thoughts of others. It allows you to overcome the feelings of sadness or upset that people often experience when they are empaths. It releases you from the victim mentality and encourages communication in a way that allows you to stand up for yourself in relationships, say 'no' when you need to, and make independent choices.
- Wintergreen- The minty aroma of wintergreen enhances focus and stimulates the body and mind. Its invigorating energies are perfect for those days when you struggle to leave the house.
- Marjoram- Marjoram is great for the skin and it is commonly used in massage oils. It helps promote a state of balance and calms the entire body and mind.

- Jasmine- Though jasmine is most well-known for its pleasant scent and use as an aphrodisiac, it also helps create balance in the emotions. This makes it a good choice for empaths who struggle with finding balance, or who may struggle with mental conditions like anxiety and depression.
- Neroli- Neroli is ideal for use after being out in busy public areas. It is an antidepressant, sedative, and brings about a sense of balance. It also counteracts the effects of anxiety, shock, and hysteria. If you have trouble clearing your mind to sleep at night, neroli oil is a good choice to add to a diffuser in your bedroom or your bath before going to bed.
- Myrrh- Myrrh is considered the oil of the earth, allowing it to create a deep grounding connection. It is a good choice when you expect to be around a lot of different energies, such as when you are going to work, school, a party, or the grocery store. Myrrh oil is also known for connecting you to a heightened state of spiritual awareness. You can apply it to your feet, over your wrists, or near your heart.
- Oregano- Oregano oil is useful for empaths who need to set boundaries. It also reduces parasitic energy and works to cleanse of negative energies.
- Eucalyptus- Eucalyptus has mood and energy boosting abilities. It improves your focus and enhances the senses.

- Vetiver- This essential oil is deeply grounding. It has an earthy scent that connects you to nature and helps bring about a state of balance.
- Melaleuca (Tea Tree)- This type of oil is useful for protecting yourself from relationships with energy vampires, or people who drain you of your positive energies. It can help you call your energy back when it has left your body for someone else's. Wearing melaleuca oil can help.
- Rose- Rose promotes a clear head, reduces mental fatigue, and can balance hormones. It also works as a general mood enhancer. The effects that rose oil has on the mind also makes it ideal for periods of meditation and self-reflection.
- Ylang-Ylang- This oil should be used sparingly to bring about a state of relaxation. It helps with problems like insomnia, depression, and anxiety. Though it is good for relaxation, it can be very strong and only a little bit is needed.
- Sandalwood- Sandalwood has deep grounding abilities and is especially beneficial for empaths who struggle with masculine energy. It also brings about a state of balance to your moods. It is commonly used for meditative purposes.
- Cedarwood- This has a woodsy, warm aroma that can be comforting. Its earthiness also promotes grounding.

- Lemon- Lemon oil has a bright, refreshing scent. It can help lift your mood and also has cleansing properties, which can help eliminate negative energies.
- Frankincense- Frankincense benefits the mind by clearing it of cluttering thoughts and conflicting energies. This ability lets you turn your focus on your own emotions and benefits concentration. It also has an uplifting effect that can stave off negative energies and depression.
- Wild Orange- This oil is a good choice when you are feeling bummed or down after experiencing negative moods. It has a slightly sweet scent and is stimulating, uplifting, and energizing.
- Sage- Sage connects with the feminine energies of the earth and is known for its shielding abilities. This is a great choice for beginners who might not be good at shielding themselves from the energies of others yet.
- Clary Sage- Clary Sage is both euphoric and sedative. It promotes hormonal balance, works to relieve insomnia, and can bring about balance for moods. It is a good choice for empaths that struggle with anxiety and/or depression.
- Lavender- Lavender is among the most versatile of the essential oils. It is most well-known for its sedative effects, as it is a common additive in bath and body products, baby lotions, and relaxation mists. Lavender

works by relaxing the mind, making it ideal for empaths that struggle with anxiety. It also clears negative energy and balances the emotional body instantly.

Chapter 8: Having Successful Relationships as an Empath

Navigating relationships as an empath comes with a unique set of challenges. When you care for someone, whether romantically or in a platonic way, you become closer to them and are more sensitive to their emotions. This makes it important to set boundaries, communicate your needs, and learn how to shield yourself from someone's energies even when you are close to them. This chapter will teach you the many secrets to having a successful relationship when you are an empath.

Communication and Balancing the Throat Chakra

The two most beneficial chakras for empaths are the root chakra and the throat chakra. The root chakra, as you will learn in Chapter 6, promotes a sense of grounding and helps you get in touch with your inner emotions. In relationships, it is extremely beneficial for empaths to get in touch with their throat chakra. The throat chakra promotes communication, which is something that many empaths have trouble doing.

Why Communicating is Important as an Empath
Communication is important in any relationship—even if you are not an empath. However, when you are an empath, communication is important to stop you from feeling drained, exhausted, and obligated in

relationships. While some people crave togetherness in a relationship, empaths require a certain amount of space. This space is necessary for them to find their center and get in touch with their own emotion. This need for spaces only increases with the amount of intimacy, as many empaths experience the strong emotions of the people they are close too even when they are not in the immediate area.

To have a healthy relationship, it is necessary to find the balance between togetherness and space. Strengthening the throat chakra also strengthens your ability to communicate your needs. This is true of romantic relationships, as well as relationships with friends, co-workers, and family members.

How to Strengthen the Throat Chakra
Strengthening and balancing the throat chakra is all about resolving any conflicts or imbalances that may exist. Often, the throat chakra is affected by past life and karmic circumstances, unresolved conflicts, blockages or damage to the throat chakra, or chronic negative behavioral problems. You can often tell that the throat chakra is imbalanced when you have difficulty communicating, pain in the neck and shoulder area, are either shy/timid or excessively talkative, impediments with hearing or speech, or blocked creative flow, to name a few things. There are several strategies that you can use to strengthen and encourage the use of the throat chakra, including:

- Caring for your throat by resting it and drinking plenty of water
- Lying on your back and consciously focusing on relaxation of the throat, neck, and jaw
- Expression through creative exercises
- Conscious effort to stop judging others and yourself
- Use of the throat, including chanting, humming, vocalizing, and singing
- Use of free expression of your thoughts, emotions, and ideas
- Regularly speaking your truth
- Gargling with salt water to cleanse and soothe the throat
- Journaling to express your thoughts

Be Clear About the Things You Need

Have you ever been at a party for a friend, but been overwhelmed by the surprising number of people that showed up? You may have felt obligated to stick around for the celebration or to congratulate them, even though you are feeling irritated and overwhelmed by all the people that have shown up. When you do finally get to interact with your friend, they may pick up on your irritation and assume you are mad.

In situations like these, it is important that you take the time that you need, whether to step away, ground yourself, and return, or simply to leave the party for the evening. If you do need to step away, take time to go to the bathroom or a spare bedroom and meditate for a few minutes. You should also drive your own car if you are going to a party or other obligation. This gives you the freedom to leave when you are ready. When you are ready to leave, approach your friend to let them know you were there. You can be honest with them about feeling overwhelmed by the number of people. If you don't feel comfortable being honest, let them know you are not feeling well and need to leave. The people who value your friendship/relationship will understand that there are times when you need to care for yourself.

Another part of being clear about your needs is learning to set limits, even with the people that you care about most. For example, it is natural to want to be there for our parents, siblings, and best friends, especially when they are going through a hard time. The strong connection that empaths share with the people they care about can make it exhausting to listen to their problems, regardless of how important the other person is to them.

It is true that not everything that happens in life is positive. It will not be your decision to fire your coworker that never finishes their part of the work. What you can do, however, is refuse to do their work for them just because they have slacked off and don't want to work over the weekend. It is also important to set limits when you are helping people work through problems, even when you are especially close. For example, imagine that your best friend or your mother is going through a rough time. Rather than neglecting them completely, explain that you can talk to them about their problem—but only for 15 minutes (or as long as you feel comfortable). If they cannot respect this, have an excuse ready to change the subject or get off the phone. Set an alarm if you need to, so that you commit to ending the topic of conversation. As you learn more about what you can and cannot handle before becoming overwhelmed, learning to set boundaries will make life easier and more pleasant.

Have Somewhere You Can Retreat

When you live with people, such as a significant other, roommates, or other family members, it is important to have an area that you can retreat to when you are feeling overwhelmed or need to spend time reconnecting with your own feelings. This could be an office, a large closet, or a specific area in your bedroom. Set up an area with things that help ground you, whether it is a photo of a place that calms you (like the beach) or a collection of crystals. For this place to be an effective area to retreat, it is important to communicate with the people you live with that you do not want to be disturbed when you are in this place. By setting boundaries, this will be somewhere you can retreat if you are feeling tired, feeling vulnerable, or need to escape from a situation. Stay in this area until you feel your heart and mind realign with your inner self. If this space helps you calm down, consider taking a photo of it and carrying it with you. You can pull the picture out whenever you are overwhelmed and visualize yourself in that area whenever you are upset.

Learning to Manage Conflict as an Empath

Empaths have a natural tendency to avoid conflict, as they do not like the surge of negative emotions that come with it. However, as empaths learn more about grounding and controlling their emotions, they actually excel at managing conflict. Empaths understand other people's true intentions and their needs, which makes it easier to reach a solution that works for everyone.

To succeed in relationships, it is important to learn how to manage conflict and disagreements.

Chapter 9: Additional Tips for Thriving as an Empath

So far, the strategies provided in this book have taught you simply how to get by as an empath. The focus has been on survival, rather than thriving. As an empath, you have a unique gift. Though it is easy to see your extra-perception of the world as a curse, it gives you a unique skill set that can be used to improve your life. You have the ability to persuade and understand on a deeper level than others. This improves your relationships, gives you insight into your own perception and the perceptions of others, and helps you solve problems, to name a few things. This chapter will teach you how to use your empathic abilities to excel.

Identifying Yourself as an Introverted Empath or an Extraverted Empath

One characteristic that differentiates empaths from others like them is whether they are introverted or extroverted. Understanding the distinction between these two types of empaths allows you to have greater insight into the things that can help rejuvenate you and charge your natural energies. There is no one-size-fits-all way to recharge your energies and bring you back to your 'normal' state of energy. While relaxing on your own is encouraged, the right type of stimulation is also needed. This helps you find that perfect balance between chaos and boredom.

The reason the needs of introverted and extraverted empaths are so vastly difference boils down to the sensitivity of dopamine that the person experiences. All empaths need to set aside time to recharge dopamine, which is the hormone in the brain most closely related to feelings of pleasure. By inviting pleasure into your life, happiness will follow. Introverts tend to recharge their dopamine levels best on their own, doing an activity like coloring, reading, meditating, or doing puzzles. As introverts are sensitive to dopamine, they do not require the same external stimulation that extraverts may need to recharge themselves. Empaths who are extraverts find themselves in need of external stimulation to increase dopamine levels, which can be a hard balance to find before you learn to block the energies of others. Some good sources of external stimulation might be going for a run with your dog or going to a concert (if you can focus on the positives and block out the negatives). The key is learning to ground yourself into whatever activity you do, so you know you are not overwhelming yourself with the experience of others. Remember to focus on your own entertainment and enjoyment.

Know Where (and When) to Find Information and Support

As an empath, one of the biggest thoughts that you will have to overcome is the belief that you will have to make it through life on your own. Scientists have come a long way in understanding highly sensitive persons and the way that their brain perceives the outside world differently than the other person. Additionally, the Internet has made it significantly easier to find support groups and literature on empaths, so you can find the support you need and a deeper understanding of what it means to be an empath.

The biggest challenge to finding these resources is narrowing down all the information and groups available, as they are not all created equally. If you type the word 'empath' into a search engine, you are going to be bombarded with different types of results—from informational articles and help resources to forums and chat groups where people can ask questions and share their empathic experience. Do not psych yourself out by becoming overwhelmed by some of the content posted—keep in mind that many of the people asking questions and sharing their experience have also had their share of struggles with being an empath.

Should you decide to do additional research online after reading this book, you should be aware that not all the information you will find is relevant. Some of the results may be unappealing or even upsetting, however, some people's view of empaths falls into the realm of fiction and fantasy, rather than the characterization of someone being highly sensitive to the environment around them. You cannot always find information you can trust online. Fortunately, using these tips can help you narrow down your search results until you find reliable sources:

1. Use Forums Wisely- Some people have especially negative experiences as an empath and may want to share or ask advice. However, not every empath experiences life the same way. Additionally, forums may have good advice, but they can also reinforce the negative side of being an empath. If you tend to focus on the negatives, you should avoid forums until you are in a better place empathically. They can be a good place to connect with other empaths and ask questions once you want to reach out, however.

2. Avoid Sites About Emotional Vampires and Psychics- Even though science has come a long way in helping people understand the empathic experience, not everyone has caught up. There are many websites, groups, and informational articles that relate to empaths as more of a psychic or 'magical' experience, rather than one experienced by people who are sensitive to their environment. Additionally, the connotation of an emotional vampire describes an empath that uses their abilities to manipulate and prey on the emotions of others. This does not describe all empaths—just the ones who use their powers for 'evil' instead of good.

3. Use Caution When Meeting Other Empaths- It may seem obvious that you should not meet up with just anyone that you have met online, regardless of how long you have been talking to them or how good your instincts are. Instead of seeking out individual empaths, look for nearby groups that you can meet up with or join. If you do choose to meet an individual, you should meet them in a public place, tell someone where you are going, and take other safety precautions.

4. Turn to Reliable Sources for Information- You cannot trust everything you read online, especially when it comes to a topic like empaths that has not been fully explored, studied, or understood. Anyone has the power to create a website, post content and photos, and make their information seem legitimate. When you dig around for information online, be sure to find information that has been written by well-established empaths, psychiatrists, doctors, and researchers.

5. Know the Best Place to Seek Information- When you are trying to understand more about your empathic nature, you should turn to scientific sources like scholarly papers and articles with psychological or scientific origins. If you are looking for support, it is best to look for help articles written by psychological websites or well-known empaths. You can also find support groups online, both those that exist in an online community and those that have meetings face-to-face. You'd be surprised how many empaths might be trying to connect in your city—they

just lack the social skills to put themselves out there in public.

6. Fact Check Everything- You should always fact check information on the Internet. Even when it comes from a reputable source, new information is discovered, and facts change as researchers' understanding increases. By staying up-to-date on the latest findings regarding empaths and how to manage life as an empath, you constantly find new insight into your sensitivity and find ways to improve the quality of your life.

Avoid Crowds When You Are in Public

Even once you have become especially skilled at shielding yourself from the emotions of others, the energy required to put a shield up can quickly wear you out if you are in the middle of a crowd of people. When somewhere is busy, make it habit to stick to the sides instead of being in the center. You can make something like a date or a dinner with friends a lot more comfortable by sitting against the wall, so you can see the door and avoiding areas that might have an overwhelming smell, like the kitchens or bathroom. If you are at a party, instead of navigating your way through the middle of the crowd, find a less-crowded room and a group of 1 or 2 people to chat with. Simply by adjusting the way that you deal with crowded environments, you can be more at ease and have an easier time shielding yourself from unwanted energies.

Avoiding External Triggers

It is not always the presence of large crowds that trigger an episode of overwhelming or unwanted feelings. It is not uncommon for some empaths to be triggered by light, sounds, smells, or other powerful external stimuli. This is the reason that some empaths avoid concerts or other brightly-lit settings where they do not have a lot of control over their environment. When you do venture to a location or gathering that might trigger a negative emotional response, take a moment to scan the location for possible issues. Avoid areas like the trash can and bathroom if you are triggered by smell. If you are at a restaurant and being around a lot of people bothers you, do not sit by the kitchen where the waitstaff will constantly be running in and out. Instead of standing by the stage at a concert where the speakers will be loud, and the light will be intense, stand toward the back of the crowd.

Decide if Medication is Right Cautiously

One common problem that empaths face, especially when they are adolescents, is the use of medications to control their empathic abilities. While there is a time when medication is appropriate, most doctors do not consider the person's heightened sensitivity before they make a recommendation for medication. Empaths are sensitive to not only their physical environment but the things they choose to ingest.

Of course, there are empaths that can benefit from the use of medication, especially if they are having trouble blocking out overwhelming feelings like anxiety and depression. Medication is most beneficial when it is balanced. Empaths who take too strong a dosage may find themselves disconnecting from regular society and unable to form healthy relationships because they lose their ability to feel the world around them. There is nothing wrong with emotions—they are part of the human experience. People who do not feel them may have trouble making moral decisions or forming mutually-beneficial relationships.

The best advice if you do decide medication is to start with a small dosage. You should not jump into the same dose of an antidepressant or anti-anxiety that the average person takes. Instead, start smaller. You can always ask your physician to increase the dosage if it ends up being too much. If you start with too great a dosage, however, you may have trouble adjusting it later.

Choose the Right Type of Job

Another obstacle that empaths commonly face is finding a job that is not overwhelming. Many strikeout in the job world when choosing entry-level positions, especially since industries like retail and food service require interacting with hundreds or thousands of people every day. In any workplace, there is also a necessity to work with people who may or may not have good intentions, from the average coworker that slacks off to the manager that constantly criticizes everyone's work.

To be a successful member of society, it is important to maintain a job. That can seem like an impossible feat for empaths who have trouble blocking out the emotions of others. Like anything that you do as an empath, however, you can easily find a job that you can thrive in by choosing jobs that exemplify your strengths without overwhelming you. For example, some empaths thrive in positions where they can use their healing nature, while others work well as leaders and members of management or human resources. Empaths that excel at healing may choose to work as surgeons, doctors, dentists, veterinarians, or in another caring position. However, if you get easily attached to patients, you may not want to work in a field where there is a high risk of coming into contact with trauma. Social work or working as a therapist also suits some empaths, particularly those who are good at helping people work through emotional trauma. Here's a list of some positions you might consider as an empath, as well as what makes each of them a good choice:

- Psychologist- Psychologists who are empaths have the added benefit of making their patients feel more relaxed, which can increase doctor-patient communication. They also can understand a patient's needs better because of their depth of understanding and help the patient build a support system, by helping explain to their family and friends what they need to be well. There is a wide range of job positions that a psychologist can hold, including working exclusively with children, in clinical settings or a private practice, at rehab facilities, or in mental health centers.

- Nurses- Holding a nursing degree is a good choice for empaths who want to use their healing nature. They excel because of their ability to help patients relax and relieve their pain, whether mental or physical. Nurses who are empaths can also help comfort patients and the people who support them. They may be employed in hospitals, physician's offices, schools, and nursing homes. Some empaths also may excel in-home care, which has fewer patients but still allows them to promote healing.
- Veterinarian- The natural caring and healing abilities of empaths are not limited to humans. Empaths may work as a veterinarian or veterinary tech when they want to heal and comfort sick animals. They can also comfort the people that bring them in.
- Park Ranger- Nature is incredibly rejuvenating for empaths. While park rangers may have to deal with people occasionally and enforce laws, most of the job involves being outside in nature. This gives you plenty of opportunities to practice your grounding abilities.
- Wildlife Rehabilitator- As with working as a veterinarian, this position is great for empaths because of the healing nature they have across all species. They can nurse animals back to health and nourish baby animals that have been abandoned by their mothers. Additionally, wildlife rehabilitators commonly work in the wilderness and this can help you

find time to practice grounding and getting in touch with your inner self.
- Musician- The emotional side of empaths make them great musicians. This is because emotion is a common ground that a musician's listeners share. Whether you write lyrics or play an instrument, you can connect with an audience through music. This makes it a good choice for extraverted empaths, who may be comfortable in the right energy setting. You can make money in band and performance contests, by creating your own music, and by performing at cafes and clubs.
- Artist- People generally believe that artists have unique emotions, perspectives, and abilities to see the world around them. By transforming their unique experience onto different mediums, they create beautiful art. Empaths fit into the artist mold because their minds are deeply insightful and have heightened perceptions of the world around them. Their views of conflict and passion create inspirational pieces of art. There are many ways you can choose to make money off your work—you can freelance and create pieces by order, sell work you have previously created, find work as an illustrator, or explore other career paths.
- Writer- Empaths intensity of emotions and perceptions can be communicated through writing as well as art. They do well with creating powerful, impactful pieces, news

stories, poetry, and all types of fiction. In addition to being an author, there is the option of creating a blog, working for a newspaper or magazine, or freelance writing.

- Social Worker- People who work in the social work field have many opportunities to help—whether they work with individuals or help entire communities. Empaths best suited for this position are those who have control over their abilities, as they cannot become emotional in tough situations. Keeping a clear and focused mind is also important. Empaths excel in this position because of their ability to understand difficult perspectives. Additionally, they can offer the support, comfort, and reassurance that the children and adults social workers commonly work with need.
- Life Coach- Empaths have many qualities that people need in life coaches, including a sense of what people need to succeed and a trustworthiness that makes clients believe they have their best interest at heart. Life coaches can work with people in a less-emotional setting, especially if they are focused on helping someone achieve their fitness or education goals. Life coaches often work privately, though others are employed by companies that connect them with clients.
- Teacher- The average empath's ability to understand the needs of people they work with make them great teachers. They typically

understand the things their students need to help them excel and they are great at helping others reach their goals. As a teacher, empaths also have the ability to impart important connections and motivation that many students need to succeed. This is especially true of students who do not receive that support at home. If you have ever heard inspirational stories about a teacher, then you understand the profound effect that teachers can have on the children and adolescents they teach.

- Guidance Counselor- Empaths excel as guidance counselors for the same reason they excel as teachers and social workers. They have an innate ability to understand the needs of others and they have the ability to know what students need to excel—be it help with homework, motivation, or help with their social life. As a guidance counselor, there are unlimited opportunities to help steer students down the right path.

Before you consider taking on a job, be sure to consider the negative side of things. Think about how even though it may feel great to work as a veterinarian, you may also deal with animals that never get better. People also commonly bring their pets to the vet when they are near the end of their life and needing euthanasia. When working in human resources, it might become required to terminate someone's employment or give them negative feedback, which some empaths might have trouble doing if they cannot block out the other person's emotions. While there are benefits for empaths and opportunities for them to use their abilities in all the positions above, most of them also come with disadvantages that should be considered. Think about the job successes and failures that you have had in the past, then use what you know to find the perfect position.

Avoid Holding onto Grudges

As empaths tend to feel things stronger than most, they may also hold onto grudges after they feel someone has wronged them. Feelings like anger and resentment can become toxic when you hold them inside, especially as you take on additional emotions from the world around you. Grudges can be compared to a poison—they run rampant in the body and have the potential to make you sick. The reality is, however, that this poison does not harm the person who has done wrong. Instead, you are harming yourself by holding that grudge and the other person may not even realize they have upset you. This makes forgiveness an important trait for empaths to develop. Even when you struggle to understand why someone has harmed you physically or emotionally, you should try to let these emotions go. If you must, channel your empathic abilities and consider what their intentions were.

In addition to forgiving others, it is important to remember to forgive yourself. The sensitive nature that empaths have can make it easy for them to be critical on themselves, blaming them for not helping more or when something goes wrong in their life. Empaths may also feel guilty or ashamed of their reactions to the emotions they feel. For example, they may become short-tempered with their spouse because they sense their child's anger at the time. Instead of being critical, learn from any mistake that you have made and allow yourself to be forgiven. Make it habit to let go of those things that do not promote a happier, healthier state of well-being.

Chapter 10: Nurturing Your Inner Empath

As you continue to grow, you'll find that there are things you can do that make your empathic abilities stronger. You will have more control over when you sense and respond to the emotions of others. You will also find yourself more in tune with yourself and the world around, able to manage conflicts better and understand what you need to be well. By continuing to nourish your inner empath, your empathic abilities will continue to grow. This chapter will teach you about overcoming the fears that hold you back, as well as how to harness your powers to invite happiness and a greater sense of success and fulfillment into your life.

Why You Should Nurture Your Inner Empath

When people are first learning to control their empathic abilities, they may think they do not want to learn to enhance them. This can be intimidating, especially if you have not had a lot of positive benefits or experiences because of your empathic nature. However, learning to nurture your inner empath does not mean that you are going to feel more of the outside world. Instead, it gives you the ability to focus on your own thoughts and feelings, as well as tune into another person's thoughts and feelings at will.

This enhanced ability to focus lets you block out the emotions of the people around you, aside from your focus (be it another person or yourself). As you continue to use your abilities in this way, you will develop many of the skills that experienced empaths have, including:

- Diplomacy- The connection that empaths share with other people allows them to understand them on a deep level. Within seconds, they can understand someone's emotions, intentions, motivations, insecurities, and worries. This deep connection allows them to sense what the people around them need, giving them the ability to engage with others in a way that makes them receptive to their message. This makes them good negotiators and debaters. These abilities are enhanced by the empath's innate ability to detect lies and predict responses.
- Charisma- People often feel drawn to empaths, being magnetized by their energy. This charismatic personality makes people 'like' you more, whether in the work environment or socially. This makes them easier to convince and interact with. You may also find it easier to persuade them. The natural charisma of an empath also helps maintain long-term relationships and friendships.
- Trustworthiness- The natural, open vibrations and calming energy put out by the typical empath make people see them as trustworthy.

Empaths are more likely to get people to open up, which is the reason that some go into fields like social work or healthcare. This trustworthiness also makes empaths excellent choices for management. People feel confident that they will look out for the best interests of the employees and the organizations, so they are more likely to follow their lead.

- Crisis Management- Once you can shield yourself from the panic of everyone around you, you can become very adept at crisis management. The heightened sensitivity of an empath's mind gives them the ability to quickly process information. Since they are natural leaders and know how to respond in a crisis, they can direct in a way that reduces confusion and chaos. This helps people get to safety quicker in an emergency.
- Healing Abilities- The empath's ability to take on the emotions of others allows them to heal both emotionally and energetically. By reading the emotions of others, they can respond in a way that lets them remove the negative vibrations away from others. This can relieve physical pain, bring friends or family members together after a disagreement, or give someone the support they need to work through a traumatic experience.

Overcoming Fears

Empaths hold themselves back in life by avoiding situations that make them uncomfortable. Even though you should take strides to make yourself comfortable and meet your own needs, it is also important to step outside of your comfort zone. This is the only way that you will overcome fears and continue to grow. Here are a few strategies you can use to help overcome fears that empaths commonly struggle with.

#1: Find a Creative Outlet
Highly sensitive people are usually too stressed about the world around them to realize the creative energy that flows between their inner selves and the world around them. This creative energy makes empaths great musicians, writers, chefs, and artists. The key is finding what you feel passionate about and then using that inner passion to drive your focus.

By expressing themselves in a creative way, empaths can find a channel to let out their emotions. As you channel creative, intense, emotional energy, you are absorbing strong emotions and releasing them as an art form. This can help you overcome the fear of absorbing strong emotions. The key to this is transforming the energy without letting it become you. Let it inspire creative works of art—visualize those energies leaving your body as you put energy into a sculpture or channel it through the movements of your hand as you write, paint, or draw. If you sing or play an instrument, imagine those passionate energies moving away as sound. As you do this, you will realize that you have the choice to either absorb or transform these strong emotions, letting them flow from you without attaching themselves and affecting your inner self.

#2: Get in the Habit of Making Your Own Decisions
Empaths are the type of people to 'go with the flow'. They might be open to social outings or a small lunch, but they are almost never the one who makes that decision. Part of gaining more control over your life is learning to turn your focus away from the outside world and look inward, considering the things that you want and need. By learning to focus on yourself, you will find yourself engaging in more activities that make you happy or passionate.

The great thing about changing your decision-making process is that it is as simple as starting to make small changes for yourself. Buy that t-shirt or dress without asking your significant other or best friend if it looks good on you. Think about if you like the piece of clothing—and then buy it. Instead of asking your friend, coworker, or significant other what they want for lunch, make a suggestion. Decide what your family is eating for dinner and what you want to cook, instead of catering to everyone's needs. Pick what movie you go see on your next date. Not only does making these decisions give you greater control in your life, but you are also going to learn more about the things that you like and dislike, rather than hoping to bump into an enjoyable time while exploring other people's decisions. Making decisions is also a useful tool in exerting yourself, which becomes important to practice as you learn to voice the things that you need more.

#3: Seek Challenges
It is easy to be intimidated by the world around you, especially if you have struggled with being an empath in the past. You may even have a subconscious aversion to places and situations that have made you feel uncomfortable or overwhelmed before. For example, you may have had a bad experience going to the company picnic or office holiday party, so you make an excuse when it comes around every year. You might want to contribute to society by doing something like feeding the homeless but have felt awful or affected when walking by someone less fortunate on the street.

However, it is important to remember that the negative experiences you have are not caused by the experience, but your reaction to it. For example, when you are doing something like volunteering to help feed those less fortunate than you, focus on the positive part of the experience instead of the negative side. Do not focus on how the person you are serving may be in pain or struggling. Instead, focus on the feelings of warmth, happiness, and nourishment that the person may be experiencing because of the warm meal they are receiving. Feel the joy of the other people that are working with you, helping to serve people who are less fortunate.

By doing things that have previously made you uncomfortable and looking for a positive experience, you change the way that you feel in the situation. It becomes a positive, healing, and wholesome experience rather than one that is filled with sadness and pain. This technique can be applied to many different situations in your life. Make it habit to seek out those situations that have tested your boundaries before. Then, use your grounding techniques and what you know about choosing the emotions you experience, allowing you to grow your empathic power and giving yourself free range of the world. The more that you push your empathic abilities, the more positive experiences you will be able to invite into your life.

Choose Your Life

One of the reasons that people hold themselves back is because they find themselves floating along with whatever life throws at them. There are times where you have to respond to life's situations. However, you should not look at life as only a series of responses. You have the potential to choose and create the life that you have, as each decision that you make brings you closer to or farther from the life that you live. You have the power to choose to leave a job that makes you miserable for one that is more fulfilling. You can make choices like this among your friends, in your romantic relationships, and in any other area where you are not satisfied with life.

The biggest challenge when making changes is knowing what to change and knowing what parts of your life are healthy. This is true of everything from relationships and employment to what you choose to do with your free time. The harsh reality that many people face in their life, not just empaths, is that not every person you encounter and every situation you find yourself in are meant to be permanent fixtures in life. As you grow, it is important to recognize and distance yourself from the things that do not contribute to your overall wellness and help you reach your goals. As you evaluate different areas of your life, consider which things make you feel bad and which harm your mental health. Try to see the whole picture and where that person or situation fits into your life. Then, decide what role these people and things should have in your life. If you have a friend that you care about but that is extremely negative, you do not necessarily have to cut them off together. If they are not committing anything to the relationship, however, you can limit the amount of time that you spend talking to them and in their physical presence. If large crowds bother you, invite friends over to hang out at your house or get a small group together elsewhere. Choose a quieter, more relaxed setting instead of a loud, raucous party or a club setting. You should also try to choose friends and relationships based on whether the person tries to see the good in others, or if they over-emphasize or focus on flaws. Cultivate relationships with people who have a mainly positive outlook—they are the people that will bring happiness into your life.

Another way to foster positivity in your life is to consume uplifting media. Choose songs that are positive and upbeat. Choose works of art to decorate your home that spark joyful emotions. When you read and consume television or movies, choose topics that make you happy or content.

Tuning into Specific Feelings

One of the benefits of being an empath is truly understanding others on a deep level. As you advance your abilities and learn to shut out the world around you, you can also learn to feel a specific person's emotions. This is a talent that takes most empaths years to master, so do not be worried if you do not pick up on it right away.

Tuning into a specific person's emotions is most effective when you are emotionally close to someone. Over time, your empathic abilities align with someone's specific vibrations. This is the reason that some empaths feel the emotions of people they care about even across long distances. For example, they may have a knot in their stomach and know something is wrong with their mother—only to find she had a car accident a few hours later. In addition to working with people that you are emotionally close to, this technique works well when you are physically close to someone. Ideally, this strategy is best learned when you are physically close to someone you share a deep connection with. Since you are already receptive to their vibrations, picking up on their energies will be easier. Once you form this connection, you will find yourself able to tune in across far distances.

The purpose of learning to tune in and tune out of someone's emotions at will is to give yourself the opportunity to focus on their feelings and needs, as well as to let you tune out and focus on your own feelings, so you can think rationally in the situation. The first step to opening the channel of your empathic abilities is to create a receptive space in yourself for that person's specific vibrations. Sit somewhere where you can be alone the first few times that you practice and meditate, taking deep breaths as you close your eyes and attempt to clear your mind. Then, imagine that roots are growing from your body and into the earth, creating a sense of grounding as you become self-aware of your own emotions and flow of energy. As you continue to feel the vibrations of your own inner core within you, choose something that will anchor you to the earth. This might be an image or an action as simple as pinching your thumb and forefinger together to help remind you that you need to return your focus to your own emotions. This will stop you from being lost in the other person's experience, rendering you unable to help them.

As you think of your anchor, sink deeper into your groundedness. Begin by relaxing the different areas of your body—beginning with the toes, feet, and ankles and then moving up to the calves, knees, and thighs. Then, feel as your fingers, hands, wrists, and arms relax. You should allow this to continue through your hips and abdomen, up your back and shoulders, and feel the relaxation of your torso, neck, and head. As your entire body relaxes and becomes heavy, feel your connection to the earth deepen. Once you reach this state of relaxation, imagine a giant anchor floating through your mind and holding you to the earth. You can pinch your thumb and forefinger together to help conjure this anchor in your mind if you are having trouble focusing on it as well. Keep focused on your anchor, noticing how your body feel as you breathe deeply, relax completely, and imagine your body dissolving until only your self-awareness is left lying on the ground.

Once you are completely grounded and aware, begin to open yourself. Imagine that you are a tree, with your roots continuing to hold you to the ground while your upper half blooms with branches, leaves, and flowers, like open arms waiting to receive what is to come. Focus on a single thought of peace or calmness as you do this and open yourself to receive that thought. After you have mastered the meditation of being receptive to calmness and peace, practice opening yourself to others and making yourself receptive to their vibrations. If you find yourself feeling lost or overwhelmed by their feelings, remember your anchor and allow yourself to return to a state of groundedness. As you learn to master this technique, you will be able to focus on a single person and know what they are feeling, thinking, and experiencing. You will understand their intentions and their needs. Once you have this information, you can use it to respond in a way that helps comfort or heal them. This can help in situations where people need to heal from their trauma, be it physical or emotional. As you learn to do this with people you are familiar with, you will feel the power start to grow over time. You will be able to respond to people you are close with against long distances and you will find yourself able to channel the pain and trauma of strangers you choose to be receptive to as well.

Using Positive Affirmations

Self-affirmations invite the things that you would like into your life. Science shows that the simple act of believing what you are stating causes you to act the way that you believe you are. By acting this way, people start to treat you as if you are what you believe you are. This can create the perfect foundation for change.

When you state self-affirmations confidently, you invite the belief that good things and positive experiences will come into your life. This almost works the same way as water molecules are drawn together—like molecules that share the same vibrational energy are attracted to each other. The belief part of the system works like this:

Imagine that your empathic nature has caused you to have several bad experiences in the workplace. As a result, you feel like you are unskilled at your job and you tend to shy away from bigger projects. Management and other coworkers have stopped asking you for help with presentations because they can see your lack of confidence in yourself. If you begin to use self-affirmations that state your confidence, you will notice a change in the way that you act at work. As you convince yourself that you have confidence, you will start to speak out more at work. You will share your ideas, contribute more, and possibly volunteer to help with a project that you might have avoided previously. As your coworkers see your confidence in your ideas and your ability to contribute to projects at work, they will also believe in your confidence and your abilities. Your actions will continue to reflect this. You will notice that you stand taller, speak clearly and look at people when you converse with them, and have a firmer, more confident handshake. You will find yourself able to share ideas, take the lead, and give presentations in a way that you would not have been previously. You can completely change the world that you live in—simply by affirming that it is different.

As you learn to change the way that you interact with the world, self-affirmations can also give you a goal to focus on. As you begin each day with the things that you want to happen, you will be focused on making those things a reality. Reciting self-affirmations is as simple as creating a list of the things that you wish to be true about yourself, your relationships, and your life. Tape this list next to your bathroom mirror. Each morning, stand in front of the mirror and state the things on that list. Look yourself in the eye as you say each affirmation in a voice that is confident, sure, and believable. If you do not believe the affirmation the first time that you say it, say it again. Continue to repeat each affirmation until you feel them resonate with you and they feel as if they are part of your inner being.

- I am loving. I am positive. I am strong.
- I embrace the reality of my emotional, spiritual, and physical wellness.
- I have the power to clear any stress or negativity in my body.

- I treat myself lovingly and value my sensitivities for their benefits.
- I embrace my empathic gifts and will explore my abilities.
- I appreciate who my empathic nature allows me to be.
- I protect myself from draining people.
- I have the knowledge to decide what relationships are healthy and set boundaries with others.
- I have the power to say 'no' at the right times.
- I care for and nourish my physical and spiritual bodies to grow into the best version of myself.
- I embrace my sensitive nature and give myself the time I need to recharge.
- I will listen to my dreams and honor my intuition.
- I am balanced and well.
- I am strong and capable.
- I have the confidence I need to succeed as an empath.
- I am a master of my empathic abilities and techniques that help me be the best version of myself.

If you have something specific that you want to focus on or change, you can also keep that affirmation written down. Pull it out of your pocket or wallet periodically through the day, reciting it in your head or aloud. It does not matter where you say it, but it does matter how you say it. Remember to state each affirmation with conviction, authentically believing that you are stating the truths of your life.

Nourish Your Body

The main focus of this book has been nourishment of the mind and soul. It is important to remember, however, that every part of your body, mind, and spirit are connected. As it is important to keep your brain sharp and well-rested to be able to focus your energy and put up shields throughout the day. The foods you eat can also have an impact on how well you function. This does not mean that you should diet constantly. Instead, focus on choosing foods that are full of nutrients. Choose healthy, fiber-rich grains, beneficial oils, and vitamin-and-mineral packed fruits and vegetables to add to your diet. By nourishing your body, you will find yourself better prepared to face the challenges of each day.

Conclusion

As you have read this book, hopefully, you have realized that being an empath does not have to be a negative experience. Many empaths grow into successful individuals, learning to work closely with people or animals in fields that they love while nurturing their inner gifts. By choosing to do things like invite positivity into your life, you can change the reality of your perception. This will help you find happiness where you once struggled with problems like anxiety, depression, and difficulty in relationships.

As you use the techniques provided in this book, remember that your goal should be achieving your own perfect balance. Each empath is as unique as their fingerprint. By learning how much stimulation you need to be happy, deciding when to experience the emotions of the people around you and when to shield yourself, recharging your energies when you need to, and nurturing your body and mind, you can change the reality of your life.

Finally, keep in mind that changes do not happen overnight. It can take weeks before you learn to shield yourself from the world around you and even longer to learn how to focus on specific emotions. However, every step that you take is a step in the right direction. By keeping yourself recharged and using the strategies provided regularly, you can lead a better, happier, and more productive life.

Best of luck!

Manipulation

Guide to Manipulation Mastery Using NLP Techniques, Persuasion and Mind Control

Daniel Patterson

© **Copyright 2018 - All rights reserved.**

The contents of this book may not be reproduced, duplicated or transmitted without direct written permission from the author.

Under no circumstances will any legal responsibility or blame be held against the publisher for any reparation, damages, or monetary loss due to the information herein, either directly or indirectly.

Legal Notice:

You cannot amend, distribute, sell, use, quote or paraphrase any part of the content within this book without the consent of the author.

Disclaimer Notice:

Please note the information contained within this document is for educational and entertainment purposes only. No warranties of any kind are expressed or implied. Readers acknowledge that the author is not engaging in the rendering of legal, financial, medical or professional advice. Please consult a licensed professional before attempting any techniques outlined in this book.

By reading this document, the reader agrees that under no circumstances are the author responsible for any losses, direct or indirect, which are incurred as a result of the use of information contained within this document, including, but not limited to, — errors, omissions, or inaccuracies.

Table of Contents

Introduction 7

Chapter 1: An Introduction to NLP,
Persuasion and Mind Control 10

    What is NLP? 10

        The Two Main Principles of NLP 11

        A Brief History of NLP 13

    What Does Learning Persuasion and Mind
    Control Have to Do with NLP? 16

        You Have a Greater Understanding of the
        Human Experience 16

        You Can Break Down the Communication
        Barrier 19

        You Gain the Ability to Manipulate 20

    The Ethics of Manipulation and Mind Control 21

Chapter 2: Benefits of Mastering NLP,
Persuasion, and Mind Control 28

    Increased Ability to Learn 29

    Increased Ability to Handle Mental Problems 29

    Heightened Awareness of When Manipulation
    Techniques Are Being Used on You 30

    Better Ability to Evaluate Relationships 31

    You Can Excel at Work 31

    Better Ability to Persuade 32

    Greater Empathy 32

    Greater Control Over Emotional Reactions 33

Increased Ability to Meet Your Goals 33
Greater Self-Confidence 34
Increased Ability to Read People and Build
Relationships 34
Chapter 3: The Basics of Neuro-Linguistic
Programming 35
Presuppositions 35
Basic Principles of NLP 36
NLP in Action 38
Terminology- An Overview of NLP Techniques 39
    Accessing Cues 40
    Changing Your Mindset 42
    Content Reframe 43
    Context Reframing... 44
    Deletion vs. Distortion vs. Generalization.............45
    Perceptual Positions 46
    Overlap 47
    Other NLP Terminology and Techniques That
    are Useful to Understand 47
Chapter 4: Using Persuasion 57
What Exactly is Persuasion? 58
Persuasion Techniques...59
    Reciprocity 59
    The Scarcity Principle 60
    The Ellsberg Paradox 60
    Hot-Hand Phenomenon 61
    Social Influence.. 62

- Commitment and Consistency 63
- Using Authority 65
- Mimicry.. 66
- Anchoring 68
- The Likability Principle 69
- Use of Sensory Words.. 69
- Choosing a Persuasion Technique 70

Chapter 5: Mind Control Techniques 72
- Entering a Suggestible State of Mind 73
- Mind Control Techniques 76
  - Active Mind Control 77
  - Passive Mind Control... 77
  - Anchoring 78
  - Anchoring in Practice: Creating an Anchor to a State of Peak Brain Functioning.........................82
- Protecting Yourself from Mind Control Tactics of Others 84

Chapter 6: Mastering the Art of Manipulation.. 88
- Knowing Your Target 88
- Use the Home Court Advantage 90
- Pay Attention to Your Physical Appearance 91
- Become a Language Master 92

Conclusion 94

Introduction

When people hear the word 'manipulation,' they often associate it with negative connotations. It may be seen as shifty or shady in nature, or an undesirable trait for someone to have. However, manipulation is not always something that must be done out of a place of ill intentions. Manipulation can be described as simply as understanding human behavior and the human experience in a way that lets you persuade and convince others. It does not have to have negative or malicious intent—some people are even manipulative without realizing it.

Have you ever considered how much easier life would be if you could do things like convince your boss that your business proposal is a worthwhile investment? Or if you could calm down your spouse and persuade them of your opinion when you disagree about parenting? Or if you could convince people to work together on a project to reach a mutual goal? Or if you could convince the man or woman you see every day at your local coffee shop to go on a date with you?

There are any number of times in your life where knowing techniques like NLP, persuasion and mind control can help you manipulate people in a way that persuades them of your ideas. This is a useful ability and it does not have to be one with bad intentions.

The information provided in this book will guide you through the knowledge, techniques and strategies that you need to learn the master art of manipulation. As you learn neuro-linguistic programming, you'll find a deeper understanding of the way that humans interact with one another and the role that language and thought have on behavior. This will serve you as you learn the best way to alter behaviors, in yourself and in other people. You will also learn about strategies of persuasion and mind control. All these techniques will come together to form a foundation that allows you to manipulate others and bend them to your will, helping you succeed at the things that you want in life. Whether you need help convincing your own mind to stop thinking so negatively or change self-destructive behaviors, or you are trying to sway someone of your opinion or to help you accomplish something, this book will lay the foundations to do that. Through continual practice, you will find yourself better prepared to face (and overcome) the challenges of the world.

Best of luck as you embark on your journey to master manipulation, NLP, persuasion, and mind control!

Chapter 1: An Introduction to NLP, Persuasion and Mind Control

Neuro-linguistic programming (NLP), persuasion and mind control are all closely related techniques that help you get in the mind of someone else and convince them of your ideas. This chapter will break down what exactly each of these abilities is and how they can be used in your life.

What is NLP?

Neuro-linguistic programming is a school of thought that involves using the three most influential elements of the human experience to understand human learning and behavior. As you understand more and learn the related techniques associated with abilities like persuasion and mind control, you will find yourself capable of implementing changes in your own behavior and changing the way you interact with people to bring better opportunities into your life.

The three elements believed to have the most impact on human behavior include neurology, language and programming. Neurology describes the inner workings of the body and mind, as the brain is responsible for regulating and controlling the way that the body works. Without the signals sent out by the neurological system, humans would not be able to perform any behaviors. Language affects human behaviors because of the impact that communication has on the way that we interface with people and the world around us. Finally, programming describes the learning process and the types of models that we create in our world. It is the dynamic that exists between neurology and language, which determines human behavior, or programming.

Though NLP focuses heavily on these three areas, it is a complete school of thought. It involves not only how you interact with the world around you and your effect on other people's behaviors, but also how you analyze and understand your own behaviors. Through understanding NLP, you have the power to change yourself and the world around you.

The Two Main Principles of NLP
The NLP school of thought is based on two major principles that are believed to be true. It is these

believed principles that shape the techniques and strategies used to teach people NLP.

The first principle is the knowledge that, as a human being, it is impossible to understand reality. Your view of the world is limited to what you perceive to be true. What you see, smell, taste, feel, or hear may be the same as someone else. However, once your brain receives information about what you are experiencing, it interprets it based on previous memories, experiences, and knowledge. For every individual, their experience and perceptions of the world are completely unique. By understanding that you cannot possibly share the same experience with someone else because of the differences in your perception of the world, it becomes clear that there is a neuro-linguistic map of the world. This map is built through your interactions and interface with the world around you, as well as your unique thought patterns. Therefore, it can be concluded that it is not reality that determines the way a person behaves—it is their perception of that reality. People are either empowered or limited by their perception—it is up to them to decide which.

The second principle of NLP describes human life and the mind as being systemic processes. They are systems of information, where data is input, information is analyzed, and there is an output. Even though each person has a unique perception of the world around them, there is still a blueprint that can be used to explain the relationship between individual human bodies, society, and the entire universe that exists around them. Consider something like the butterfly effect—the phenomena that something as simple as a butterfly landing on a tree can cause an outward ripple that leads to a disaster somewhere. This interaction creates complex relationships, which is the reason you cannot possibly isolate a person's blueprint of their mind without understanding how the world outside of them and their personal views have shaped their experience.

A Brief History of NLP

The history of NLP is brief because it has been studied much less than older models of behavior and learning. The earliest work was done by Richard Bandler, who had a background in gestalt therapy and mathematics, and John Grinder, who had a background in linguistics. These men came together to create a model of behavior that they called neuro-linguistic programming to describe the relationship that exists between language, a person's interactions with the world, and their behavior.

The first work that studied the ideas that would later form the foundation for NLP was *The Structure of Magic*, which had two volumes released in 1975 and 1976. These studied the behavioral and verbal patterns of both renowned family therapist Virginia Satir and creator of gestalt therapy Fritz Perls. In separate volumes titled *Patterns of Hypnotic Techniques of Milton H. Erickson, M.D.*, which also had two volumes published in 1975 and 1976, the behavioral and verbal patterns of psychiatrist and founder of the American Society of Clinical Hypnosis, Milton Erickson.

After these initial studies were published, Grinder and Bandler continued their work, this time forming modeling techniques and adding contributions to the field. There would be several books published by the two men and other contributors, including *Frogs into Princes* published in 1979 by Bandler and Grindle, *Neuro-Linguistic Programming Vol. I* published in 1980 by Dilts, Grinder, Bandler, and Delozier, *Reframing* published in 1982 by Bandler and Grinder, and *Using Your Brain* published in 1985 by Bandler.

Even though the study in this field has been brief, the breakthroughs and understanding have been vast. There are many applications for NLP in the world today, each of them using the powerful tools and skills for sending a message and clear communication. Among the areas where NLP can be applied are parenting, psychotherapy, life coaching, self-improvement, counseling, sales, creativity, health, education, management, and law.

Most recently, the evolution of NLP has continued. The 1990s ushered in a new era of NLP, which uses a systemic approach to help people understand their true identify and achieve their mission. One of the most referenced works on the current studies of NLP is *NLP II: The Next Generation – Enriching the Study of Subjective Experience* by Dilts, DeLozier, and Dilts.

What Does Learning Persuasion and Mind Control Have to Do with NLP?

When NLP is combined with persuasion and mind control techniques, it creates a highly effective way of manipulating the people around you. As you learn more about the human mind and how it works, you become aware of each individual's unique experience. This knowledge lets you understand how they think, how they learn, how they communicate, and what internal factors influence their thought and behavioral patterns. Once you have formed this framework of understanding, you can use persuasion and mind control techniques more effectively. Instead of choosing typically-effective methods that may or may not work, you can choose a targeted approach that lets you take advantage of someone's subjective experience.

You Have a Greater Understanding of the Human Experience
Take a moment to consider that two people that had the same mental and physical ability attempted the same task. Even though it would seem these two people were both adequate for the job, one was more successful than the other. Where would the difference

lie? Neuro-linguistic programming can be described as the subjective experience that a person has. This subjective experience is unique only to them, as no single person experiences life in the same way. For example, even when two twins are raised by the same family, each may have a different interaction with their parents. This difference in interaction shapes their subjective experience, so each twin grows into an individual despite the similarities in the upbringing.

By understanding a person's unique series of steps that they go through when making the decision to do something, you can start to build a map. This is done using NLP sequences. Often, people are unaware of the many factors that influence their human experience. A behavior as simple as turning on a light switch triggers several decisions that each reflect a different part of the human experience. A sequence that describes the action of turning on a light switch might look like this:

Ve > Ad > K- > K

These letters may stand for-

- Ve- This is the visual external. It describes the initial decision to turn on a light, upon

deciding that there is an inadequate amount of light in the room.
- Ad- This is the internal self-talk an individual may have. They may think to themselves that 'it is really dark in this room.'
- K- - This is a negative kinesthetic feeling. It might be annoyance or discomfort that results from being in a dark room.
- K- This describes the final kinesthetic step of movement. It is the physical action and positive kinesthetic response that results when the light is turned on.

Most people are not aware of these processes as they happen throughout the day, as each decision and element happen within a fraction of a second. This is only one small sequence—there are thousands, even millions of strategies that humans may apply to the human experience. They simply are not consciously aware that this is happening.

With a deeper understanding of the way that the human mind works, you'll find yourself better prepared to notice and use the behavioral patterns of the people around you. As you notice these things, you will begin creating a blueprint to their mind. As your understanding of their experience grows, so will your ability to use persuasion and mind control techniques that work.

You Can Break Down the Communication Barrier

One of the problems that exist in today's society is an inability to understand the true message that someone is sending. It is not uncommon for people to focus on the verbal part of communication, that is, the words that are actually spoken. They listen to the words of other people and hope to find a meaning while crafting a response that they believe will get their message across. However, research conducted in the 1970s shows that only 7% of a person's true meaning can be understood by hearing their words. The other 93% comes from other factors—the micro-expressions on their face, tone of voice, speed of speech, and other non-verbal cues. There is also an enormous amount of communication that happens within a person—their inner mindset, feelings, and attitudes strongly influence the message they are trying to send.

By learning to understand the true meaning of what people are communicating, you can learn more about how to interact with them in a way that benefits you.

As you understand the true meaning behind someone's communication, you learn more about them and the way that they think. You might better be able to understand their needs or how to clarify your own needs. This creates a deeper channel of communication than is experienced with the average human interaction.

You Gain the Ability to Manipulate

Salesmen, psychologists, and others who may use manipulation in their line of work will tell you there is no single method of persuasion or mind control that works flawlessly, every time. They often profile the person they are speaking with, using clues from the clothes they are wearing, how their hair is groomed, the way that they speak, and their overall character to help them decide which manipulation technique is best. For example, a car salesman that is trying to sell an SUV to a young couple might notice the dog hair on their clothing and note the roomy space in the back that is perfect for hauling everything from gear to pets.

The Ethics of Manipulation and Mind Control

Manipulation, mind control, and even the simple art of persuasion has an ethical side and an unethical side. As with anything, the ethicality behind manipulation and mind control depends on how it is being used. Consider how guns may be used. On one end of the spectrum are people who are trying to protect themselves and provide food. On the other are people who may use guns to threaten or harm others. The same is true of manipulation techniques—they can be used in a way that is honest, ethical, and with good intention, or they can be used in a way that is harmful.

As you read, the strategies discussed should not be used to coerce or unethically manipulate someone in a way that alters their typical behavior. Here are a few examples of potentially unethical ways that manipulation may be used:

- The Silent Treatment- This type of manipulation is intended to put someone into a state of uncertainty. The manipulator does not verbally communicate with you or respond to e-mails, texts, calls, and other calls, even if you are being reasonable. The silence is used as leverage and they often create a condition to help ease that uncertainty once they decide to start talking to you again.

- Constant Criticism- People naturally struggle with arguing with people they see as superior, especially in the case of authority. However, this superiority can also be established by manipulators who constantly judge or criticize you. By putting you down, they are building themselves up.
- Fear and Relief- Fear is a strong emotion—just think about the last time you were terrified of something or had to face a phobia. One technique is to create a fear about something, and then come sweeping in with a solution or a way to ease the stress that was caused.
- Acting Ignorant- Being ignorant is 'playing dumb.' For manipulators, this is a useful tool when they are trying to avoid an obligation, hide something, or delay something. A classic example is a spouse pretending they do not know what their spouse is talking about when they confront them about hotel room charges

on their credit card bill or ignoring their spouse as they loudly sigh, bringing in the third load of groceries they have taken from the car.

- Guilt- Creating guilt works best in situations when the other person has done something wrong (or can be manipulated to believe they have done something wrong). Once they are in this state of mind, they will want to compensate for whatever they have done wrong—by doing the next thing suggested usually.

- Playing the Victim- The victim card is typically a favorite among narcissists, who blame the world around them for the negative things that happen in their lives. It is also commonly used with making a person feel guilty or as if they can do something to help. It is not uncommon for manipulators to use imagined or exaggerated personal issues in their manipulation, especially when they are trying to get sympathy or favor from others.

- Gaslighting- Gaslighting describes the action of creating a response in someone else. Manipulators might poke fun at someone's insecurities, say something to elicit an emotional response or be offensive in a way that makes the other person upset. Once they are upset, the manipulator only feeds the fire—then blames the person they are manipulating for the way they responded and 'starting' the problem.

- Pressured Decisions- If you have ever been rushed into a decision, then you know how hard it is to think rationally when you are under pressure. This is a common tactic employed by salespeople—they may rush you into saying 'yes' to whatever they are selling before you have done your research. It can also be employed by manipulators who are trying to get you to agree to something.
- Overwhelming with Information- If someone approaches you about a political candidate, they might be quick to start piling on the facts about what the candidate supports, who they are running against, and how their opponent is a bad person or has made poor decisions in the past. The hope with overwhelming someone with information is to overload their

ability to process everything, leaving them vulnerable to persuasion.
- Overwhelming with Red Tape- In some situations, manipulators may list all the things you have to do to accomplish something as a deterrent for that action. They may note committees to bypass, procedures that must be done, laws that are in place, paperwork that must be completed, and other things that must be done to make something possible. A wife who does not want her husband building a garage may do this by telling him that there are zoning laws, getting approval from the homeowner's association, filling out paperwork for materials, and getting a bank loan before he can get started on the project.

Even though most would agree that some of the tactics above are generally unethical, that does not mean that they are never appropriate. Consider for a moment that you had a friend with a sick child and they could not afford medicine. They want to rob a bank for money. In this situation, if you could not rationally persuade your friend to stop their behavior, would it be wrong to use guilt? Would it be unethical to tell them that they will probably get caught and then their child will not have a parent—or their medication? For most people, this is a situation where manipulation is almost necessary to prevent negative outcomes for many people involved, including their friend, their friend's child, and anyone who may be in the bank.

Since it is not clear-cut, it is important to develop a system that you can use to ethically use manipulation and mind control tactics. Before using the strategies provided in the following chapters of this book, ask the following questions:

1. What is the intention of persuading that person? What is my desired outcome?

2. Is the manipulation I am using transparent and truthful? Or am I trying to convince them by being deceitful?

3. Is there any benefit for the person I am trying to manipulate? Does it benefit anyone else (or the greater good)?

Returning to the example of the friend who wanted to rob a bank, manipulative tactics would have been appropriate. The manipulation had the intention of preventing negative outcomes, such as jail time, death, the loss of a parent, or other unforeseen results. The guilt technique is truthful and transparent being used to sway the friend's attitude to see that what they are doing is not a good solution. Finally, using manipulation in this situation benefits everyone involved, including the individual, their child, and the greater good.

Chapter 2: Benefits of Mastering NLP, Persuasion, and Mind Control

Many of the NLP, persuasion, mind control and manipulation courses you find online are going to promise near-instant results. The reality is that it takes time to understand and map the human mind. Using NLP and mind control strategies are all about progression. While you may be able to detect cues on sight that allow you to persuade even a complete stranger, you will develop collective knowledge over time. That being said, true mastery of NLP, persuasion, manipulation, and mind control techniques takes time. As with anything that takes time, it is easy to commit to the challenge when you know what you stand to gain. Here are some obvious (and not so obvious) ways that mastery of the techniques in the chapters that follow can change your life.

Increased Ability to Learn

As you understand more about the inner workings of your mind, you'll find yourself better able to understand difficult subjects. NLP benefits the learning process because it helps you understand how you learn best. According to the VARK model of learning styles, for example, people primarily learn well using a combination of visual (seeing), auditory (hearing), reading/writing, and kinesthetic (hands-on) learning. Even though most use a combination of techniques, most individuals have a strong preference for one or two of these styles. When learning complex topics, they can increase their comprehension by choosing a method that lets them use their brain's preferred style of learning. Not only does being aware of your ability to learn help you understand more, but it also increases your memory retention.

Increased Ability to Handle Mental Problems

Neuro-linguistic programming can be combined with mind control techniques for you to use on yourself. This can help interrupt negative thought patterns that are common with anxiety and depression. These skills are also useful for overcoming negative habits, overeating, and different types of addiction. This benefit comes from the approach that allows thought patterns to be addressed. For most people, changing the thought patterns is easier than simply changing the behavior. Creating new thought patterns in the brain is another part of this process.

Heightened Awareness of When Manipulation Techniques Are Being Used on You

It is not only people with good intentions who may be masters at manipulation. Some people learn manipulation easily over the course of their life, while others possess the skills of charisma, charm, and a desire to bend those around them to their will at a young age. By understanding how manipulation is done, you increase your awareness of your interactions with the people around you. You also will notice personality traits and signs that you are being manipulated. You'll learn more about these signs later in the book.

Better Ability to Evaluate Relationships

The reality is that most people do not know when they are being manipulated. You might even find there is someone in your life that is manipulating you, whether it is a relative, a friend, a co-worker, or even your significant other. By learning to recognize the signs of manipulation and NLP mind control, you can eliminate toxic people from your life. Over time, you will build a positive network of people that help you on your path to excellence.

You Can Excel at Work

People who master techniques like NLP and manipulation excel in the workplace. They often work well with teams, have an advantage when it comes to convincing prospective clients to use their services or products, and have the skills to recognize and speak on problems that exist. By sinking into your role as a natural leader, the skills provided in this book can help you interact with coworkers in a way that quickly has you moving up the ladder of your organization.

Better Ability to Persuade

You cannot completely eliminate human interactions from your life. As most people cannot avoid interacting with the people around them, at work, at home, and in the streets, it is best to know how to interact with these people. As you persuade people to help you focus on your goal (and their own), it helps propel everyone around you to excellence. This persuasion can be used to create stronger relationships, excel in the workplace, try new things, and more.

Greater Empathy

One of the benefits of understanding NLP is that it gives greater insight about the human experience and how it shapes perception. In addition to understanding how your own mind works, NLP gives you insight into how others' minds operate. This means that while you cannot possibly put yourself 100% in their shoes and understand their exact situation, you can have empathy for their situation.

Greater Control Over Emotional Reactions

Emotional reactions often seem instant. Have you ever received sudden news and felt a powerful surge of emotion running through your body, not even a second later? When you learn the way that the mind works in triggering that emotional response, you learn how to better control the way you react in different situations. This gives you power in times of stress and can help you hide your emotions when you need to. For example, you may want to appear strong at work even though you are going through a personal crisis.

Increased Ability to Meet Your Goals

The major point of mastering manipulation and NLP is to become the best version of yourself that you can be. By mastering the techniques in this book, you will learn how to convince people to help you meet your goals. You will also learn how to convince your own mind to help you reach your goals, by achieving a state of excellence. With your body, mind, and the people around you all compatible with what you are trying to achieve, you will find there is nothing in life that you cannot do. You will be able to meet goals in all area—from academic and career goals to those based on physical fitness and your personal life.

Greater Self-Confidence

As you continue to meet goals and learn more about your strengths, you will develop greater self-confidence. Additionally, you will find yourself better prepared to deal with the things that do not make you feel confident. This includes understanding your flaws and why they may exist, as well as taking the steps to overcome them. This greater self-confidence will flow into all areas of your life. You will learn to speak up in relationships that do not suit you and have the confidence to pursue the people you are interested in. You will also have the confidence to take on more challenging projects at work (and succeed).

Increased Ability to Read People and Build Relationships

As you learn more about NLP and manipulation, you will start to notice how people's appearance, gestures, and other non-verbal communication sends messages about who they are. This will give you the ability to persuade even when meeting someone for the first time. You will also have the ability to lay the foundation for relationship building, even shortly after meeting someone. This helps create connections that will be helpful, in both your personal and professional life.

Chapter 3: The Basics of Neuro-Linguistic Programming

Though neuro-linguistic programming can be used to understand the unique experience of others and how it affects their perceptions of the world, many of its applications have to do with the individual. In theory, it was founded as the study of 'human excellence.' Among its many applications include helping people reach goals, overcoming psychological disorders like depression, anxiety, and phobia, and increasing personal performance in all areas of life. It can help people excel romantically, at work, or in their day-to-day life.

Presuppositions

Presuppositions are central principles or assumptions that people have generally formed based on their life circumstances. Presuppositions greatly affect the way that something is perceived. As the subconscious mind receives information from the five senses, it filters it using information from past experiences.

This is how a person's core values, beliefs, and attitudes are shaped, and it is through this filter that they view the world.

Even though presuppositions are determined by the subconscious mind, it is possible to grow the size of the mind map. Even though NLP focuses on understanding the current map that exists, that does not mean that new territories cannot be explored or that the existing pathways cannot be changed.

Basic Principles of NLP

1. Failure does not mean you have failed—it just means you have not succeeded in your first attempt. Failure should not be viewed as something that limits your future exploration of something. Instead, it should be viewed as an opportunity to learn from mistakes and find out what works.

2. Keeping a positive mindset is important. When you believe something has happened that limits you, take a moment to be grateful for a choice. In some situations, there is no opportunity for choice (or change) at all.

3. Remaining flexible is key. It gives you the opportunity to try new things when something else

isn't working. It also stops you from being limited by the choices and options presented to you in life.

4. You are not limited by anything. Even when someone has an extraordinary skill, talent, or ability, the fact that it is possible for them to accomplish something means it is possible. If it is possible, then anyone has the potential to learn it.

5. Communication elicits a clear response. It is important to communicate effectively if you want to share your thoughts and ideas. This includes verbal communication, as well as your body language.

6. To effectively use NLP in your communications with other people, it is important to learn to respect their personal view of the world. Without understanding and using your model, you may come across as abrasive or unlikable. This will not be beneficial to your goal, especially if you are trying to earn their trust or convince them to do something.

7. To understand behavior, you must understand positive intentions. In the example earlier in the book where the parent considered stealing money to get medication for their sick child, the positive intention was that desire to heal their child.

8. Every person is useful. Whether you are considering your own talent or trying to understand someone else, it is important to remember that every person has value. To tap into this value, it is important to understand the person's unique talents and contributions.

NLP in Action

Let's take a look at how NLP may work in practice. Imagine that there are two people, Person A and Person B. Each of these people is shown a snake. While Person A is terrified of the snake and experiences a rapid heartbeat and shaky palms, Person B is comfortable with the snake and has a desire to hold it. It is clear that Person A has a problem with the snake—they may have had a toy snake that scared them when they were a child and only remember it subconsciously, or perhaps they were bitten by a snake. Regardless of the reason, their mind map and the way they perceive snakes is different from Person B.

To overcome the fear of snakes, NLP might help Person A associate positive words with a snake. As these positive associations become programmed into their brain, it changes their mind map and the way that their brain perceives snakes. Over time, they may pair the positive terminology with positive experiences, like getting enjoyment from watching a snake and eventually holding a snake.

By helping people overcome phobias, giving people with learning disabilities the unique approach and tools they need to learn, helping in self-improvement, encouraging personal growth and excellence, helping someone excel in happiness and wealth, and doing many other things, NLP can be used in many fields. It is used effectively in the business world, teaching, psychotherapy, sales, life coaching, and much more.

Terminology- An Overview of NLP Techniques

The mind is a complex and vast place. To understand the depth of the mind, and to learn how to expand and change your mind map, it is important to understand some of the ways that NLP can be used. As you understand these, you will find a deeper understanding of the motivations and the perceptions of others. You may also start to see connections between language and thought that exists within that person's mind.

Accessing Cues

Accessing cues describe information that your appearance relays about the brain's pathway to information. The most common research done has been on eye accessing cues, which was discovered by Grinder and Bandler after several workshops. The movement of the eyes occurs in patterns when the mind is accessing information. Interestingly, a person's dominant hand determines what it means when their eye's shift when looking for information.

For a right-handed person:

- The eyes going up means that they are visualizing
    - Up and to the left means images are being constructed
    - Up and to the right means the images are being remembered
- The eyes going straight and defocused also means the person is visualizing
- The eyes moving side to side on a horizontal plane indicate that the person is hearing sounds or words
- The eyes moving to the left indicates remembering

- The eyes moving to the right indicates creating
- When the eyes move down and left, it indicates that an internal dialogue is being experienced
- When the eyes move down and to the right, it indicates the person is in kinesthetic mode, meaning they are more aware of physical sensations, movements, and feelings

For a left-handed person:

- The eyes going up means that they are visualizing
    - Up and to the right means images are being constructed
    - Up and to the left means the images are being remembered
- The eyes going straight and defocused also means the person is visualizing
- The eyes moving side to side on a horizontal plane indicate that the person is hearing sounds or words
- The eyes moving to the right indicates remembering
- The eyes moving to the left indicates creating

- When the eyes move down and to the right, it indicates that an internal dialogue is being experienced
- When the eyes move down and to the left, it indicates the person is in kinesthetic mode, meaning they are more aware of physical sensations, movements, and feelings

The key to using this information is understanding that each retrieval of a thought or memory is only one part of the process. Chances are, someone's eyes will move in several directions before they answer a question or say something to you. These movements may be subtle, so it is important to pay attention.

Changing Your Mindset

One technique of NLP uses frames, which are conscious states where you are asked to re-evaluate information or an assumption. The most commonly used frames include the as-if frame, the backtrack frame, and

The as-if frame of mind instructs a person to act that something they wish to be true is. Rather than focusing on how you cannot do something, it is helpful to frame things in your mind as if you are good at that task. For example, you might be able to overcome your lack of confidence when learning something new by framing your mind, so you can think of things 'as-if' you were skilled in that area.

The backtrack mindset requires you to go back over information. This is done the way you would rehash notes following a meeting. It gives you time to process the information and think it through. Rather than assuming you interpreted it correctly while you were still receiving the information, being in the backtrack mindset lets you slow down and analyze what you have heard. When other clues are noticed, you might find the information is different than how you originally perceived it to be.

The outcome frame requires you to visualize the desired outcome. By thinking about what you are going to achieve, you give your mind the opportunity to re-evaluate what you know and what you need to do to reach the desired outcome, whether it be meeting a goal or remembering specific information.

Content Reframe
This strategy describes the conscious effort to change the way your mind thinks about something. It involves asking questions like "What haven't I

noticed?" or "What else could this mean?". Questions like these reframe, helping you redirect your focus and giving a wider range of options when analyzing content.

For example, imagine that you walk by a coworker that always smiles at you and greets you in the morning, but they are staring at the floor and oblivious to the world around them. Instead of assuming that coworker is upset with you, it might be useful to reframe the content and consider what else could be happening. Is it possible they are under a lot of stress or are dealing with a painful experience? Could they just have been distracted that day?

Context Reframing

While content reframing analyzes specific statements and situations, context reframing analyzes behaviors. Instead of focusing on the behavior specifically, the context and meaning behind the behavior are considered. It is the 'why' of the behavior rather than the behavior itself.

Context reframing is very useful when trying to build mind maps as you do during NLP because more than one behavior might be caused by an underlying context. For example, someone who is irritated when around crowds may not be in a bad mood—they just might feel anxious. By understanding that this irritability is caused by anxiety and not being moody or upset, it may also explain the person's irritability in other situations when they are anxious, like when giving a big presentation.

Deletion vs. Distortion vs. Generalization

These are the three processes that make up the Meta Model of Learning; deletion, distortion, and generalization.

Deletion describes when part of the experience is left out. This can be applied to the repression or altering of bad memories. In the case of a phobia, for example, even though the mind may delete or repress the details of the traumatic experience, the connection to the trauma still exists. That is why the mind still experiences anxiety and other phobic reactions when exposed to certain stimuli.

With distortion, the mind believes something is true even if it is not. This has to do with perception and it does not always occur intentionally. For example, someone may see a curly strip of rubber tire on the road and assume that it is a snake when the reality is that it is a piece of tire.

Finally, with generalization, the mind relates a single, isolated experience to an entire group. One common phenomenon that can be used to describe this is ageism, where people assume that people may not be capable of doing something because of their age. For example, older people might be considered bad drivers while it may be assumed that people who get pregnant at a young age are going to be bad parents.

Perceptual Positions

Perceptual positions describe a person's view of the world. It is often referred to as your Model of the World, as well.

First Position describes a state where you are only in touch with your inner model of the world. In this frame of mind, you have a limited viewpoint.

Second Position is the place you put yourself in for second-person point-of-view. This allows you to see the world from a specific person's point-of-view. It is similar to the saying, "Put yourself in somebody else's shoes."

Perceptual Position describes the point-of-view you would have as an uninvolved observer. It allows you to see only the facts of the situation and takes away from bias and emotional involvement.

Overlap

The overlap strategy is used to create an overlap between the information that you already know and what you are trying to access. For example, imagine that you are trying to access information that you would understand using the sense of smell (olfactory), but your preferred representational system is kinesthetic. You might visualize yourself walking (kinesthetic) down the beach and hearing the birds. Then, you feel the course, cool wet sand as it squishes under your feet. You smell the saltwater and are transported back to the memory of your wedding on the beach.

Other NLP Terminology and Techniques That are Useful to Understand

- Accessing Cues- In addition to eye movements, accessing cues include other external signals that give clues about someone's internal thinking process. This includes patterns in posture, gestures, and breathing as well.

- Anchoring- This technique can be used to create a specific response in someone. The mind is programmed to respond in a certain way. This may occur naturally in someone with a phobia—seeing the thing that scares them triggers their anxiety. We will talk more about how to put this technique to practice in the chapter on mind control.
- Associated- Associations are a major part of NLP. The associations that your mind creates ultimately determines your perceptions in life. It describes your auditory, kinesthetic, and visual relationship to what is going on outside of you.
- Behavior- Behavior is the external action that can be verified. It is sometimes referred to as the external verifiable.
- Complex Equivalence- This describes the idea that two statements mean the same thing. For example, someone may link the statements "My spouse is angry at me" and "My spouse didn't smile at me when I walked in the door" because they believe the two are related.

- Congruence- This occurs when a person's external verifiable matches the words that they say.
- Conscious- The conscious describes what a person is currently aware of. It is their experience and the part of the mind where they can 'hear' themselves think.
- Contrastive Analysis- This is used when comparing and analyzing two Sub Modalities for information that makes them different. For example, someone who does not like yogurt but loves ice cream, which are both sweetened dairy products, may compare and contrast them to see what in their mind is driving their dislike for yogurt.
- Crossover Mirroring- This is the combination of using a physical movement with an external behavior, matching the two even though they are not related. For example, during a hypnotic session, a therapist might move their finger to simulate the physical act of the client breathing.
- Deep Structure- The deep structure of a sentence describes the unconscious meaning behind a statement. It is the underlying

framework behind someone's statement and considers its context outside of conscious awareness.

- Disassociated- Disassociated describes your relationship to an experience. For example, you may look at a memory but see your body instead of seeing it through your own eyes. This represents a disconnect somewhere.
- Downtime- This describes a time when the conscious goes inside of the mind. This is where you can go to connect with internal bits of information and your true feelings. Information collected during downtime is incredibly useful for building a framework for the mind and understanding connections.
- Drivers- Drivers are the reason behind forming the connection. They represent reasoning, intent, and purpose.
- Ecology- Ecology describes the consequence aspect of decision-making. When you decide something, there are several consequences on your own self, as well as your business, family, others involved, society, and even the planet as a whole.

- Elicitation- This is commonly used in mind control techniques to induce a certain state in a client. It may also be used to describe the act of gathering information from observing client behaviors or asking questions.
- Epistemology- This is the study to determine how people know the things that they know.
- Incongruence- An inconsistency between a person's words and their behavior.
- Internal Representations- This is the content of our thoughts in its entirety. In addition to the information we receive from the senses, it includes self-talk that we consciously include. Internal representations are also sounds, pictures, feelings, smells, tastes, and emotions that we create.
- Leading- Leading is a tactic useful in manipulation and persuasion. It involves changing your behavior in a way that the person you are interacting with changes their behavior. For example, someone might reduce conflict by leading with a calmer approach.
- Lead System- The lead system describes the connections that exist in the brain. Essentially, the pathway that we follow in the brain to find

certain connections lies within the lead system. The series of patterns that your eye makes while accessing information determines where it is moving through the lead system.

- Matching- Also called mirroring, this technique is used to mimic someone else's emotion. The mimicry makes us seem more like the other person. As people have a general 'like' for themselves, they like people who are similar to them. This is useful for gaining a rapport and establishing trust, especially when you are persuading someone.
- Metaphor- NLP often uses metaphors to help people understand specific information. If they have a subconscious aversion to something, by using different words but making a different connection, the resistance to the words being used can be bypassed.
- Meta Model- The Meta Model of language is used in NLP to recognize distortions, deletions, and generalizations. It also helps you build the tools necessary to clarify imprecise language.
- Milton Model- The Milton Model is used in NLP to help people reach their unconscious

resources. It often relies on abstract language patterns that are ambiguous to your life experience.
- Model Operator- This is used to describe word relationships that define different parts of our lives. The Model Operator of Possibility applies to words that represent the possibility of something, such as can and cannot. The Model Operator of Necessity describe words that relate to the rules we fall in life, such as have to, must, and should.
- Parts- The parts discussed in NLP are conflicting values in the mind, which are stored in different 'chunks' of information. These conflicting values account for incongruences in behavior.
- Preferred Representational System- This is unique to each person. It describes their preferred method of thinking. It also helps them organize experiences within their brain.
- Resources- In NLP, the resources being described are the means and strategies that every person has to accomplish their desired outcomes and create internal changes. This

includes changes in states, strategies, beliefs, attitudes, values, and physiology.
- Resourceful State- A resourceful state is one where a person has helpful, positive strategies and emotions at their disposal. This heightens the chance of whatever the desired outcome is being successful.
- Sensory-Based Description- A description based on the senses should do so without making assumptions about the other person's state of mind or allowing our minds to alter perceptions. Rather than assuming someone is happy, for example, you would say that their mouth is curved upward at the ends and they have a symmetrical face.
- State- State describes a certain awareness of the mind or an internal emotional condition. A state may be something like being in a suggestive state of mind or being aware of your presence. It can also be an emotional state, such as being in a happy, angry, or sad state. NLP also focuses on achieving a state of excellence, which the peak of your mind's functioning.

- Surface Structure- Surface structure is the base meaning of a statement or how it is intended to be received based only on the words. It leaves out the context and understanding that comes along with the deep structure.
- Time Line- Another possible approach of NLP is Time Line Therapy, which makes use of the timeline. Essentially, the timeline describes memories of the past, present, and future. With Time Line Therapy, the goal is to release the negative memories and associations to stop limiting decisions, with the eventual intent being the creation of a more positive future.
- Trance- Trance can be used to describe any altered state of mind. For the purpose of hypnosis, NLP, and mind control, it is commonly used to create a single-pointed inward state of focus.
- Unconscious- The unconscious, or subconscious, describes the state of your mind when that you are not aware of. It is the area where memories are retrieved and perceptions are created.

- Uptime- Unlike downtime, uptime describes a state of mind where you have an outward focus.

By developing an understanding of the different NLP techniques and how they can be used, you begin to develop an understanding of what you need to know to become a master manipulator.

Chapter 4: Using Persuasion

There are two types of persuasion that are commonly used to sway someone's attitude or beliefs—persuasion that appeals to emotion and persuasion that applies to logic or rationality. Though persuasion is generally considered less 'threatening' sounding than manipulation, it can be just as effective. In fact, as persuasion generally uses a gentler approach, the effects may be longer lasting than those of manipulation. Generally, persuasion requires a shift in attitude. Students are taught how to write persuasive papers, where they rely on facts and concrete ideas to support their thesis and persuade the reader of their opinion. It is a change in attitudes and beliefs, which happens on a deeper level than manipulation.

The goal of persuasion is to use either the heart or mind to sway someone. The salesman mentioned earlier that persuaded the couple by mentioning how they could haul their pets around was appealing to their mind and the romantic vision of living their life with their dog in tow. Someone trying to convince a loved one to eat better, join an exercise program, or quit smoking my appeal to their mind by casually pointing out the benefits of doing those activities over time. Another technique may be to appeal fear—by exercising regularly, the loved one might be able to avoid hospitals (which they hate). This chapter will go over some of the most common persuasion techniques. These are useful when trying to pitch an idea or product, arguing a point, or otherwise trying to reach the desired outcome.

What Exactly is Persuasion?

There are several elements that make communication an attempt at persuasion. It is a symbolic process that involves someone attempting to convince another person or group to change their beliefs or attitudes. For this to be considered persuasion, and not manipulation or another technique, the message to change the beliefs or attitudes has to be in an atmosphere that leaves the person free to choose.

Though the definition of persuasion has remained the same over the years, people's exposure to it has increased dramatically. On average, an adult living in the United States is exposed to the persuasive messages of between 300 and 3,000 advertisements—and that is only through their media consumption. That does not include the messages they are receiving from their significant others, people at work, and others they encounter through their day. While some advertisements may use persuasion tactics that are obvious, others have started to use a subtler approach. In addition to subtlety, complexity is also needed to help the message reach a wide range of people. This is what makes knowing your target audience so important.

Persuasion Techniques

Reciprocity

The principle of reciprocity describes the innate human behavior of giving something back when we receive something. This is the reason that political groups might send out free pens, stickers, t-shirts, or other 'gifts'—they are trying to raise donations. It is also not uncommon for websites to give out free copies of an e-book to convince visitors to sign up for their email list.

For the principle of reciprocity to be most effective, you should give and then try to persuade soon after. This can be obvious sometimes (such as when asking for donations). However, since the person has already accepted your help or what you had to offer, it is often effective even when the persuasion technique is obvious.

The Scarcity Principle

The idea behind the scarcity principle is that there is limited availability of something. To be included in the hype, someone has to make a decision about being included—fast. You could use this to convince clients to try new software you are test-driving or to convince friends to make plans with you—telling them that you are available only 1 or 2 nights in the following couple weeks, but that your schedule is filling up fast, can make them more likely to make plans with you before you are unavailable.

The Ellsberg Paradox

The Ellsberg Paradox takes advantage of the human mind's natural dislike for uncertainty. The idea of this paradox comes from experiments carried out in 1961. For the studies, the test subjects had to choose from two urns that had been filled with a combination of red and black balls. The first urn contained an unknown ratio of the red and black balls, while the second urn contained fifty of each number. The subjects then were asked to choose an urn and guess what color would be drawn—those who were correct would receive $100, while those who were incorrect would not receive anything. Participants overwhelming chose the second urn, with a 50-50 chance of winning, rather than taking the unknown risk of going with the first urn.

This study represents the human's mind unwillingness to take risks when they are unnecessary. By creating the risk of uncertainty, you make people more likely to be swayed by the next best option. Once they are in this state, you can convince them of your 'solution.'

Hot-Hand Phenomenon
The Hot-Hand Phenomenon describes the subconscious belief that people have 'winning' streaks. Generally, when someone does well at something, it is expected they will continue doing well at it. This is explained by the common saying, "Success breed success." It also describes why people in sports like basketball commonly pass the ball to the

same player. Even though statistics show that no player has ever made 100% of their shots, they assume that the person who is on a winning streak for the game will continue to make winning shots. You can capitalize on this persuasive technique most effectively after someone has experienced a win of sorts.

Social Influence
The social influence strategy involves using the influence of someone's peers to sway their attitudes or beliefs. Social influence, or social proof, relies on the way that behaviors, opinions, and emotions are influenced by the people around you. This works in several ways. Humans are naturally social creatures, so they like to have the confidence of their peers. To be seen as 'normal,' to fit in, and to be like the people that they admire or like, they are more likely to share attitudes, behaviors, and opinions with the people close to them.

Think about the way that a teenager is often pressured to ask for their first cell phone. They may protest if their parents say 'no,' insisting that all their friends have one. If you are trying to get someone's interest, it can be beneficial to introduce the topic in a way that their friends might agree with. For example, introducing the idea of vegan leathers to people who have eco-conscious friends. Testimonials are another common way for people to be convinced to do something. Think about the way that anti-aging, weight loss, and other beauty products commonly have before and after photos, proving that they work among someone's peers (people who struggle with the same problems as they do).

Commitment and Consistency

As you learned in the chapter on NLP, the human mind relies on patterns to help it understand the world. The world around us is built on a series of patterns and our mind relies on patterns to store, access, and interpret information. This is the reason that people have trouble changing hardwired belief. For example, politics is an area where it is hard to sway people about their opinion. Often, they will go to great lengths to either prove their team are the greater candidates for the job or discredit the other team. It is human nature to want to believe we have made the best choice. As we reassure ourselves, we consciously decide to continue on whatever path we have chosen.

This technique is most often used by introducing just a small part of an idea first. Some of the earliest research on the commitment and consistency principle was carried out by Jonathan Freedman and Scott Fraser in the mid-1960s. A 'volunteer' researcher went door-to-door in a neighborhood and requested that they could put a large sign in their yard. The sign was poorly designed with amateurish lettering and stated, "DRIVE CAREFULLY." They were unsuccessful in convincing most homeowners, having just 17% agree to have the sign placed. For the second part of the experiment, a similar neighborhood was chosen, and the researcher went door-to-door again, this time requesting to place a small sign that read, "Be a safe driver." Almost all the homes in the area agreed to placement of this 3-inch sign. When approached two weeks later by the same researcher, who asked to put up the larger sign, 76% agreed to it. This is a significant amount higher than the first research group. The reason the tactic was more effective was that the homeowners wanted to remain consistent in their commitment to promoting safe driving.

Using Authority

People are more likely to do things for those who they see as authoritative figures. This is the reason that people comply with people like the police and children listen to teachers and their parents. One of the most famous studies conducted on authority was carried out by Stanley Milgram. Participants were invited to the lab to help with a 'learning' experiment. At the beginning of the experiment, two people were introduced and drew straws. The 'learner' is taken into a separate room, strapped to a chair, and attached to electrodes. The electrodes were connected to the electricity in the other room. The other person played the role of the 'teacher' and followed instructions given to them by the experimenter, a man in a gray lab coat.

The learning portion involved the teacher giving a word and then having the learner recall the partner to create a pair from a list of different choices. Each time the learner gets the answer wrong, the level of voltage on the machine is turned up and they received a shock. There were thirty clear-labeled levels, ranging from a slight shock of 15 volts to a button that was labeled 'Danger- Severe Shock' at 450 volts. The learner intentionally got the answer wrong and was then 'shocked.' The shock was faked, but the teacher was unaware of this.

Through the experiment, when the teacher eventually stopped and questioned the morality of the experiment, 1 of 4 prods was used. Even though some of the teachers showed reluctance, all of them obeyed the experimenter and continued to a level of at least 300 shocks. About 65% of the participants continued beyond this, going to the maximum level of 450 shocks.

Therefore, it stands that when you do have authority, you can use it as a persuasion technique. In addition to authority that comes from a position of power, you can also persuade using authority stemming from a position of knowledge. This is the reason when people give presentations or write persuasive papers, they try to persuade using statistics and facts. This factual information proves their credibility and their knowledge about the topic.

Mimicry
When you mimic someone the right way, it can increase your rapport, or trustworthiness, as well as liability and positive feelings. This is based on the idea

that people subconsciously respond in a more positive way to people who act like them, sound like them, and look like them.

One study that tested this idea was carried out by Cornell University's Michael Lynn. Lynn and his team assembled two groups of servers; one group acknowledged customer's orders by indicating with a nod or other simple acknowledgment and the other repeated the order back to customer's using the same words they had used when they ordered. The result showed that people preferred the servers who repeated them—they received 78% of tips from diners, while the other group only received 52% tips.

Other studies have looked at body language and gestures as well, showing that people were more likely to be convinced (or like) people who shared common movements with them. The key to mastering this technique is learning to mimic without being noticed. However, you must also mimic soon enough that the subconscious mind catches the similarity—even though the conscious mind does not. When a person moves, you should mimic their movement subtly, about 1-2 seconds later. If they touch their face, touch yours 1-2 seconds later. If they cross their legs, cross your legs the opposite way, about 1-2 seconds later. It is critical that they do not notice you doing this, however. Not only will it lead to an awkward conversation, but your mimicry will also leave them less-than-interested in whatever you are trying to convince them of.

Anchoring

The anchoring technique for persuasion involves creating a focal point to help with persuasion. You should note that this is different than the anchoring technique that will be discussed in the chapter on mind control. To use this anchoring technique, a focal point is created. For example, you may try to persuade a friend to loan you money by asking for a little more than you need. Then, when they say no, you can ask for less. Since they are focusing on the first number and know they are getting away with letting you borrow less money, they are more willing to say yes. This also works when doing something like negotiating the price of a car. If you tell someone a lower number than you are willing to pay and let them talk you up a little, you end up paying the amount you originally intended to pay.

The Likability Principle

The likability principle describes the idea that people like other people who are similar to them. This is the reason that mimicry works as a technique. In addition to using mimicry, you will also notice that people are more likely to agree with people who look like them or act like them. They are also more likely to do things for people that they like.

The likability principle is one of the six original persuasive techniques, as discussed by Arizona State University professor Robert Cialdini. It does not include just being similar, but also your level of attractiveness, your natural charm, and people's attitudes toward you in general. So, it is a good idea to dress well when you have a presentation or are trying to persuade your spouse of something. You can also make people laugh and use your natural charm to get them to do the things that you want.

Use of Sensory Words

Are you trying to create a message that stands out? Using sensory words can be helpful in helping people remember your intended message. For example, you may want to help client's use their senses to visualize the product you are trying to sell them. You might convince your spouse of a vacation by using the senses to help them visualize lying on the beach somewhere warm, feeling warm sun on their skin and the perspiration from a cold drink running down their hand.

When you use sensory words, you really help your intended audience get an idea of what you are saying. You can use similes and metaphors to deepen the understanding and help things stick. You can also use imagery to conjure up specific images and leave a lasting impression.

Choosing a Persuasion Technique

While all the persuasion techniques listed above are effective, they can only be used under the right circumstances. You cannot use mimicry if you are presenting to a large room of executives. Instead, something like the Ellsberg Paradox or another technique would be more effective.

After you have considered the circumstances and what might be appropriate, consider your intended audience. Shape the persuasion technique based on what they expect, how similar the other party is to you, and if they may or may not like you already. BY knowing your audience, you can also carefully consider word choice, body language, and other factors that are going to affect the way your message is received.

Chapter 5: Mind Control Techniques

When people think mind control, it often conjures images of thoughts being projected into someone's head or brainwashing being used. Hypnosis is another commonly used mind control technique—often depicted in Hollywood as having the power to make someone quack like a duck or otherwise make a fool of themselves. However, mind control goes much deeper than this. There are elements of mind control in day-to-day society—you'd be surprised how much television and something like 'flicker rate' has the potential to change the thought patterns of your brain. The military is also known for its use of mind control and there are implications of it in education, programming, medication use, sports, politics and many other areas of life.

Outside of manipulative practices, mind control is a useful tool for therapy. It can help people unearth repressed emotions and memories, which can help them deal with underlying issues. Additionally, it can help with overcoming bad habits and creating a more positive frame of mind, particularly one that is useful for reaching the state of excellence that is stated by NLP. While this is a form of manipulation, it can be used as a positive form of motivation that creates positive changes. So, how can you use this information, not only to protect yourself but to help improve your day-to-day life? Keep reading to find out.

Entering a Suggestible State of Mind

Whether you are performing self-hypnosis or trying to use a form of mind control on someone else, the first step is to enter a suggestible state of mind. Having the right mindset is key since being aware of what is happening will cause the mind to be limited by your subconscious. Additionally, being in the wrong state of awareness creates a resistance against certain messages.

To enter this state where the subconscious can be easily accessed and influenced, the body and the mind must both be in a state of relaxation. The goal is to create the alpha brainwave state of the mind falls within the frequency of 8-12 Hertz.

There are many types of relaxation, depending on your desired intent. As achieving this state is critical, this makes it easier for people to resist unwanted hypnosis and mind control without using modern methods. Here are a few methods that may be used:

- Progressive Relaxation- This type of relaxation involves tensing and releasing different muscles in the body, usually while focusing on a single object in the mind. This is one of the longer styles of relaxation and can take up to 30-45 minutes to induce.
- The Silva Method- Visualization is used in this technique to induce a state of relaxation. It works best in scenarios where the person being controlled would normally be relaxed. For example, you would not use a beach relaxation scenario for someone who is afraid of water. Engaging the senses is very important when using the Silva Method. With more senses being engaged, a higher state of relaxation can be achieved.
- Brainwave Entrainment- Brainwave entrainment is usually an ambient sound that is generated at a specific frequency. To induce

an alpha state, a frequency of 8-12 Hertz is projected. As the brain waves synchronize, the subconscious opens and the mind becomes receptive to suggestions. The three brainwave entrainment technologies used include isochoric tones, binaural beats, and monaural beats.

- Flashing Lights- Flashing lights have the same ability to induce certain frequencies of brainwaves in the mind as specific sounds do. The study of inducing certain states or behaviors with flashing lights is called optogenetics, which has been studied more in the past years.

Consistency and relaxation are major parts of inducing a highly suggestive state. It is important to relax the person in a way that they are not distracted by things inside or outside of them. This state of relaxation can be used to access specific memories, learn new information or habits, or create a suggestion that seems natural. Once you have induced a state of relaxation, you can move onto one of the following techniques.

Willingness is another major part of inducing a highly suggestive state. You should not use mind control on people who are not willing. You may even find that progressive relaxation does not work on people who are unwilling. It also works best on people who are not worried or afraid of hypnosis or mind control. Being informed about what is going to happen and easing tensions beforehand help induce a relaxing state.

Something to note is that relaxation and hypnosis are not the same technique. While relaxation may be useful, the person is much more conscious and aware in this state than they are when being relaxed for the purpose of hypnosis or mind control. Additionally, relaxation strategies are often induced in a way that makes participation optional and easy to slide in and out of. Mind control relaxation is usually progressive and it is hard for the person to slip out of that state without a cue or signal.

Mind Control Techniques

Once that suggestible state has been reached, it is time to make the suggestion that will create the change or decision you are hoping to see.

Active Mind Control

Active mind control involves being aware of your relaxed subconscious state. You can create changes in your mindsets, attitudes, thoughts, and behaviors, but only you are aware of what you want to achieve. Focus on your outcome. Imagine what it would feel like or look like if you accomplished your change. Then, imagine yourself stepping through a doorway and becoming that person. When you awaken from your meditative trance, you will become that person. You could also use this mind control technique to help a friend who is going through a hard time.

Passive Mind Control

Subliminal messages slip into the mind and bypass your conscious awareness. They are often slipped into relaxation music, which eases your mind and then leaves it in a state where messages can easily slip into your subconscious. This is done by making the messages so quiet that they cannot be perceived (heard) by the human ear. However, their frequency can still be detected by the subconscious.

Since you are not consciously active in this type of mind control, it requires a pre-recorded message and relaxation music. There are many varieties of this, each with a different subliminal message. Since you cannot consciously hear what is being said, it is important that you choose messages from a reputable company that will not take advantage of their customers or create mind control with an unethical intent.

Anchoring

The anchoring technique involves a behavior or stimulus that creates a mood or state of mind. One of the most famous anchoring techniques was conducted by Ivan Pavlov, who trained dogs by feeding them every time that he rang a bell. Once the dogs were trained, their mouths would salivate, and they would experience hunger pangs every time that the bell rang. In addition to creating certain reactions, this strategy can be used to create a certain mindset. For example, someone who regularly feels joy after winning on several scratch-off lottery tickets might feel joy after scratching the ticket—even if they do not win anything. The work done by Pavlov is called classical conditioning, which happens when certain behaviors, emotional states, or mental states are triggered without a conscious effort. To effectively use this as a mind control technique, anchors are used.

The best types of anchors relate to the different learning and retrieval processes of the mind, including visual, auditory, and kinesthetic.

Visual anchors work well because humans are visual creatures, especially at a young age. Think about the way that a child gets excited when they see their favorite fast food restaurant—even though they can't read yet. We might see someone's face and have our day ruined or our mood instantly change or feel joyous when we see our bank alert on Thursday mornings that always indicates our paycheck has been deposited.

Auditory anchors can also trigger certain states or behaviors in the mind, these types being associated with sound. For example, you might hear the theme song of your favorite television show coming from the other room and get excited or experience dread at the sound of the alarm clock in the morning.

Kinesthetic anchors involve physical action or touch and links it to a certain state of mind. People who experience anxiety, for example, might use a mind control tactic where they link the physical action of making a circle with their thumb and forefinger to help ground them or calm them when they are having an anxiety attack.

As anchors are created as we have specific reactions to certain stimuli and behaviors, it is not uncommon for people to create their own anchors through life. Advertisers often use this, creating commercials that induce a certain emotional state, so that whenever you think of that product, you think of it in a positive way. For the purpose of mind control, anchors could be used to induce a state of relaxation as mentioned in the example earlier or make someone quack like a duck every time that someone claps. The possibilities are endless, but there are several elements that must be in place for an anchor to a certain state or behavior to be effective.

- Intensity- At the moment when an anchor is formed, its intensity determines how quickly that anchor will be relied on in the future. It might take several times for that person with anxiety to consciously train their mind to relax when they make that hand gesture, but someone who is terrified of snakes may only need to have one bad encounter with a snake to have that state of fear induced each time they see or hear a snake.

- Timing- The most effective anchors are those created within the right timeframe. Good anchors will be created at the peak of the experience when the feelings that go along with it are most intense. Trying to maintain this state and intensity for a longer period of time will also strengthen the connection.
- Uniqueness- Creating an experience that is unique is important to avoid being triggered in your day-to-day life. You do not want to use a common sound like clapping to trigger a certain behavior or mental state—imagine what would happen if you went to a movie theater, performance, or speech.
- Replication- Replication involves your practicing of the anchor and continuing to make that association. Over time, the anchor will grow stronger. Remember that recreating the experience accurately and consistently each time is critical to strengthening the neural pathways in the mind and forming a strong, memorable anchor.

Anchoring in Practice: Creating an Anchor to a State of Peak Brain Functioning

Now, let's take a look at this in practice. This strategy can help you in times when you are having trouble focusing on your work or whatever task is at hand. Since one element of this anchor is your posture, it is important that you consistently use it somewhere you can sit tall. A desk or table and a chair will work well since this is a scenario you can easily recreate whether you are at work or at home.

If you work best with music, choose music to play quietly in the background. You could also run a fan for background noise or leave the room silent, depending on how distraction-free the area is. Once you are comfortable and in a distraction-free environment, sit down in your chair. Sit tall, with your shoulders positioned over your hips and your spine elongated enough to give you an erect posture. However, you should not stretch your spine so much that it is uncomfortable.

Once in position, breathe deeply. As you inhale, imagine yourself drawing in rejuvenating, oxygenating breaths. The oxygen from these breaths is filling your body and your mind, priming them to perform their breaths. As you exhale, all the worries of the day and anything that may distract you should float away, like bubbles or clouds that carry these things far away from you. Now, touch your thumb to your forefinger.

For the next part of this, it is best for these words to be spoken aloud. Since it may be easiest to allow them to seep in if you are in an altered state of conscious, you may want to record them on a tape and play them for yourself during that training phase.

As you sit in a state of deep relaxation, you are creating a state in your mind,

You feel calm and focused. Your mind feels strong and powerful. You are ready for the tasks ahead of you.

As you sit in this state of calm, focused intent, you bring your thumb to your forefinger and feel the connections in your mind strengthening. You feel yourself becoming more powerful.

Your mind is capable of the tasks you have for it. It is rejuvenated and awakened. You bring your thumb to your forefinger again.

Sit in this state and imagine that power filling you, as electricity fills a computer. Your mind is being recharged by the energy of your body and the room around you. You bring your thumb to your forefinger again.

Sit in this state for several moments. If you feel your mind slipping out of focus, bring your thumb to your forefinger again to reawaken this state. This transports your mind to a state of heightened awareness and processing power.

You bring your thumb to your forefinger and feel yourself awakening, ready to face the work ahead of you.

Protecting Yourself from Mind Control Tactics of Others

Imagine that you had an emergency come up for the weekend and you needed to find someone to finish up your presentation for the following week. Now, think about which of your coworkers you might ask for help. What factors determine someone who is more likely to say 'yes' to your request? You might have thought of a coworker that you helped move a few weeks earlier or who you did work for another time. Or, perhaps you thought about the coworker who is most likely to say 'yes,' simply because they are a team player. Regardless, this decision was based on who would be easiest to persuade to do the work for you.

Mind control victims are often chosen because they are easier to persuade and manipulate than others. There are several reasons that might make someone stand out. By knowing what master manipulators look for, you can also be aware of how to protect yourself from the mind control attempts of others.

People who exercise mind control on others for their personal gain are usually charming in nature. They draw their victims in with their charming personality, self-confidence, and natural ability to exert authority and appear as a leader. They know how to get people to do what they want.

These people are often overlooked because of human nature. We believe that all people have good in them, even those who have made horrible mistakes in life. This belief that everyone has some inherent good can make you a target for mind control. It is also human nature to appear polite, so if we catch someone treating us poorly or acting out, it is harder to confront the person. As the connection between us and someone strengthens, so does their power of influence.

Additionally, as humans naturally believe people are good, they may not understand why people would be hurtfully manipulative. Thinking that it could never happen to you or not understanding how it works is the first way to be manipulated. If you believe that someone may be using mind control on you, take time to consider the nature of your relationship. Have they ever been giving in a way that did not leave you feeling guilty or obligated later? Have you ever done something that goes against your core values when you were persuaded by them? Do you find it hard to be angry or upset with them? By knowing what to look for in a manipulative person, you can make yourself more aware of people who may not have your best interest in mind. Some of the signs that you may exhibit that makes you a target for manipulative people include:

- Difficulty saying no, asking questions, or expressing doubts
- Preoccupation with how others see you
- A desire to find clear answers, in a short timeframe

- Being in a state of stress, anxiety, or depression
- Substance abuse
- Superstitious personality
- Dependent personality
- Susceptibility to altered states of consciousness
- General discontentment with society

It is also common for manipulative people to target others who struggle with their lack of purpose or meaning or who have a general dissatisfaction with their life. They may feel lonely, have low self-esteem, or be experiencing a failure of some kind. There are also many positive traits that people who are easily mind controlled have, including a high regard for authority, naïve idealism, a need or desire to find a higher level of spirituality, and a caring nature or desire to take care of others. These are all traits that a manipulator can take advantage of.

Chapter 6: Mastering the Art of Manipulation

Now that you have an understanding of NLP, mind control, and persuasion, this chapter will give you additional techniques that will help you master the art of manipulation. As mentioned in the first chapter, these strategies should be used in a way to reap positive results. Always consider all possible outcomes before manipulating someone for your gain or their own. While there are times where it is appropriate, there are also times when it is unethical to manipulate someone in this way.

Knowing Your Target

The best way to manipulate someone is to gain an understanding of their unique perspective of the world. You will do this as you learn more about them over time. To have a complete understanding, you must consider the three following aspects of personality:

- Private Personality- How people experience themselves, internally. It is a collection of personal preferences, values, hopes, ambitions, emotions, thoughts, and attitudes. Private personality can also include positive and negative traits, some, which we may work toward improving, and others, which we may try to ignore or forget.
- Persona (Public Self)- How you see yourself, externally. This is the way that you wish others would see you. The public self is the conscious choice of what you reveal or keep hidden from the world around you. Generally, people try to show the parts of themselves that they think best while minimizing the 'bad' parts.
- Reputation- How others see a person, externally. The reputation is not something that people are responsible for themselves, as it involves how they fit into other people's perceptions of the world. While they may have some influence on how people see them, generally, people are judged based on first impressions and their appearance. Overcoming this first impression bias is crucial since it is common for people to look

for information to prove they were right about their initial assumptions, rather than seeking information that might make their opinions change. This is one of the reasons that people who are naturally likable are good at mind control and manipulation—even when they show signs of being manipulative, people tend to ignore it and try to confirm their first impression of them instead.

By learning these different pieces of information about the people you spend time with, you can learn more about their true interests and intentions. You will understand the congruencies and incongruences that exist between their thoughts and physical behaviors.

Use the Home Court Advantage

There is a reason that members of management like to call employees to their office when they are upset with them—it gives them an advantage. As the employee is likely to be uncomfortable or familiar with management's office, they are less likely to argue and more likely to submit to orders.

When you are trying to persuade someone, it is easiest to do it when you have the comfort advantage. For example, a co-worker is more likely to agree to help with your workload for the weekend if you are driving to lunch in your car and they are sitting passenger than they would be if they were sitting in the driver's seat. You can use places like your car, office, home, or other places where you are both familiar and comfortable.

Pay Attention to Your Physical Appearance

Once someone has judged you for the first time, they will spend the rest of your interactions together trying to find information that proves that initial impression that you left with your appearance. When you are trying to leave a positive impression, it is important to be well-groomed and appropriately dressed for the impression you want to leave. As it is best to be in power when you are trying to leave a good impression, choose clothes that make you look nice and feel powerful. Your haircut also helps determine the message you send, so be sure to choose a style that fits your face.

When you are unsure of your audience, you should not choose an outfit that might be considered a fashion risk. Choose something that fits your body well and shows your confidence. When you are not sure of what to wear, go for a classic look. Black dresses, a smart-looking skirt and blouse, and suits are all good classic pieces that nearly always make a good impression when worn correctly.

Become a Language Master

Language is a critical part of NLP, persuasion, mind control, and manipulation. To connect to a wide range of people from different life experiences and backgrounds, it is important to master language. As you learn to read people, you will learn more about the positive and negative associations that they have with certain words. By choosing those that are more or less appealing, you can create a dialogue that manipulates in a way that will allow you to achieve your goal.

There are many elements of mastering language. One of them is having a wide vocabulary range and being familiar with different dialects. Reading in different genres can help you understand communication between people. Additionally, by broadening your language capabilities by learning, you will also have the opportunity to learn more about different topics. This gives you more material to talk about and helps you speak about different topics with ease. Reading any materials can help you speak better and improve your vocabulary—from newspapers and magazines to textbooks and novels.

Working on your voice, tone, and body language can also help. Most of what we communicate is non-verbal, so it is important to send the message you are trying to. Be sure that your body language and tone align with the words you are saying. To gain confidence in your interactions, it is a good idea to practice in front of the mirror. Review scenarios you found yourself in through the day or imagine communication scenarios. Then, speak to yourself in the mirror as if you were speaking to the other person. Notice your movements and what they are conveying as you speak.

Conclusion

As you develop a deeper understanding of the mind and how individual experiences shape perceptions, you can use this information to sway people of your opinion and convince them to take action in their lives. It is important to use this information ethically, in a way that does not cause harm physically or emotionally and in a way that benefits the greater good.

Whether you use what you have learned in the workplace or in your personal life, you are now armed with the tools that you need to succeed. You will be able to convince people to support your ideas and goals. You will also be able to use NLP and mind control techniques on yourself, helping you achieve a state of excellence where you can excel.

Though many people relate manipulation to being a negative tactic, there are many ways that it can be beneficial and appropriate in your life. By combining manipulation techniques with NLP, mind control, and persuasion, you will find that life gives you the things that you need.

Best of luck!

www.ingramcontent.com/pod-product-compliance
Lightning Source LLC
LaVergne TN
LVHW010321070526
838199LV00065B/5626